RECIPES FROM MY
INDIAN
KITCHEN

RECIPES FROM MY INDIAN KITCHEN

NITISHA PATEL

PHOTOGRAPHY BY CLARE WINFIELD

RYLAND PETERS & SMALL
LONDON • NEW YORK

For the three most empowering women
I have ever and will ever meet…
My grandmother, who showed me the magic of cooking.
My mother, who showed me 'the way' with her cooking skills.
My sister, whose love, support and selflessness know no bounds.
This book is for you three.

Senior designer Megan Smith
Editor Kate Eddison
Production manager Gordana Simakovic
Creative director Leslie Harrington
Editorial director Julia Charles

Food stylist Emily Kydd
Prop stylist Jennifer Kay
Indexer Hilary Bird

First published in 2017; this edition published
in 2024 by Ryland Peters & Small
20–21 Jockey's Fields, London WC1R 4BW
and 341 E 116th St, New York NY 10029
www.rylandpeters.com

10 9 8 7 6 5 4 3 2 1

Text copyright © Nitisha Patel 2017 and 2024

Design and photographs copyright
© Ryland Peters & Small 2017 and 2024

ISBN: 978-1-78879-516-6

Printed in China

A CIP record for this book is available from the
British Library. US Library of Congress Cataloging-
in-Publication Data has been applied for.

Notes
• Both British (Metric) and American (Imperial
plus US cups) measurements are included in these
recipes for your convenience, however it is important
to work with one set of measurements and not
alternate between the two within a recipe.
• All spoon measurements are level unless
otherwise specified.
• Ovens should be preheated to the specified
temperatures. We recommend using an oven
thermometer. If using a fan-assisted oven, adjust
temperatures according to the manufacturer's
instructions.
• All eggs are medium (UK) or large (US), unless
specified as large, in which case US extra-large
should be used. Uncooked or partially cooked
eggs should not be served to the very old, frail,
young children, pregnant women or those with
compromised immune systems.
• When a recipe calls for the grated zest of citrus
fruit, buy unwaxed fruit and wash well before using.
If you can only find treated fruit, scrub well in warm
soapy water before using.
• To sterilize preserving jars, wash them in hot,
soapy water and rinse in boiling water. Place in
a large saucepan and cover with hot water. With
the saucepan lid on, bring the water to a boil and
continue boiling for 15 minutes. Turn off the heat and
leave the jars in the hot water until just before they
are to be filled. Invert the jars onto a clean dish towel
to dry. Sterilize the lids for 5 minutes, by boiling or
according to the manufacturer's instructions. Jars
should be filled and sealed while they are still hot.

Pattern on cover by katyau/Adobe Stock

MIX
Paper | Supporting
responsible forestry
FSC
www.fsc.org   FSC® C008047

CONTENTS

INTRODUCTION

Magical spice powders, sizzling funny-shaped dried spices, noisy popping saucepans, aromatic smells, colourful foods… this is what sums up my childhood: great home-cooked Indian food!

I was born and raised in Wolverhampton in the West Midlands. My parents are from the state of Gujarat located in the west of India, just off the Gulf of Khambhat. During the mid-nineties, my parents, before they had even met, had both lived and spent time in South Africa. At this time, for a 'better quality of life', thousands of families migrated from Gujarat to eastern and southern Africa. At the time, Africa was seen as the land of opportunity and an easy way to make money fast. Today, it is quite evident to see the influence that Africa has had on modern Gujarati cuisine.

From Africa, both my maternal and paternal grandparents moved to the UK and settled in Wolverhampton. In 1980, my parents met, got married and had three children; my older sister, myself and my younger brother. Growing up as part of a 'big fat Gujarati family' was an eccentric and interesting experience to say the least, but a magical one.

With a large family on both sides, there was always a family event to attend every weekend. Whether it was Diwali, Christmas, New Year, a birthday, an engagement, a wedding or just a family get-together, the family have always made an effort to meet up and enjoy each other's company. With regular Gujarati get-togethers, comes regular, large doses of different delicious delights; explosive home-cooked curries, tasty Tandoori chicken, crispy deep-fried bhajis, hand-crafted samosas, aromatic biriyanis and

so much more… To me, a family party has always meant one thing: good food – I suppose that's where my love for food comes from. I always associate good food with family, happiness and having a good time.

From a young age, I have always been interested in food. When in the company of visitors, my parents often tell a funny story about how if I was playing-up as a child they would keep me occupied by giving me a large bag of peas to pod in return for a treat. Whether it was watching my mother cook her famous lamb curry on Sundays, helping her to make her special spice blends or watching my favourite chef idols on TV, I was fascinated by the magic of cooking. Curiosity took over and I started to cook new and exciting dishes at home in my mother's kitchen.

After finishing high school, I went to the well-established College of Food at University College Birmingham to study Culinary Arts Management. From day one, I was hooked! The course lecturers were addictively charismatic and passionate about gastronomy. The courses themselves were very in-depth sessions about the hospitality industry. I had seen professional kitchens on TV but never before had I been or worked in such a well facilitated environment. Going to university to study was an absolute dream come true, even if it did mean that I wouldn't become the politician, lawyer, doctor or accountant my family thought I would be!

After four years of exams, assignments, practicals, studying and writing a dissertation, I couldn't wait to get into the big wide 'hospitality world' and put my culinary skills to use. I had been a student long enough and I wanted some practical experience. Food and cooking had now become a huge part of my everyday life and I was hungry to learn more about different cuisines of the world.

Following two years in the industry, I became a development chef for a global corporate company. The job involved tremendous amounts of research and development, and also engineering convenience products that were commercially and nutritionally viable. I was familiar with working to a budget before, but controlling the amount of calories, saturated fat, protein, salt and vitamins that were going into a product, while also making it taste beautiful, was a great challenge. The research and innovation aspect of the role involved many inspirational food trawls where I ate at some of London's greatest foodie places; from the finest Michelin-starred Indian restaurants to the very best street-food stalls.

I was constantly reading about Indian cuisine too; from some of the greatest and oldest Indian cook books to the most contemporary books by the latest celebrity Indian chef. Combining my own knowledge from what I had learned at home, with what I was reading from some very amazing cook books and what I was tasting and identifying as the latest food trend, I developed Indian dishes that were manufactured in their millions.

I gained a deep understanding of authentic Indian cuisine. I began to experiment more and more at home. All I thought about during the day would be what my next creation was going to be, what can I make at home using what I've got lying around? I started making home-cooked dishes that I would like to eat in restaurants and showed friends and family pictures of what I had made. My friends and family seemed to be quite impressed and many of them asked for the recipes – that got me thinking about writing this book, a way in which I could showcase my love and passion for the food I grew up eating.

This book is all about Indian food that is great-tasting, fresh, vibrant and guaranteed to have your friends and family impressed, too! There are a variety of recipes; some are shockingly simple, some are all about slow-cooking for minimum effort and maximum flavour, and some are really quite extravagant. The majority of recipes are far-removed from traditional 'curry-house' style dishes which have been developed for the average consumer. I don't cook dishes like a Tikka Masala or Madras at home, and so I have not included recipes for these types of dishes.

Trends show that more and more people travel around the world in search of new and exciting eating experiences. They are becoming more food curious and developing a taste for authenticity. Today, every supermarket has a 'world food' section, proving the demand for world ingredients.

In my opinion, long gone are the days where the average couple will order a curry and pilau rice takeaway on a Friday night. With so many celebrity chefs and foodie shows on TV, most people prefer to cook their own food. The only problem is convenience, and in today's busy society, how many people have the time to prepare a freshly cooked meal every day?

This book offers authentic meals, most of which won't take as long as a curry to cook but will still deliver the same flavour punch, and equal amounts, if not more, of a fun, impressive meal experience.

MY MODERN INDIAN KITCHEN

You can probably imagine how ingredient-packed my kitchen is – I am very fond of trying any new ingredient and wandering into grocery stores to see what's new that I haven't tried. Having an Indian background means that I have a huge amount of dried or ground spices and seeds lurking about, but having a corporate job means I am all about the convenience! Long days in the office can only mean one thing when it comes to dinner – I want something quick, convenient, healthy and tasty all at the same time. Before we get to the recipes, I have created a glossary of the main ingredients used in Indian cuisine.

SPICES

Rumour has it that Indian food is spicy. Yes, this can be true, but it can also be quite the contrary too! Indian food can be as spicy as you want it to be; spice levels vary from dish to dish, from region to region and from occasion to occasion. The key is getting to know your spices and therefore getting the balance right! Of the hundreds of spices there are in Indian cuisines, each plays a different role and adds a different level of magic to your dish. I always categorize my spices into whole dried spices, dried spice seeds, spice powders and fresh spices.

WHOLE DRIED SPICES

Asafoetida Digestive aid, flavour enhancer, harmonizes all flavours, extremely strong scent.

Bay leaf, dried Distinctive flavour and fragrance, pungent with a sharp bitter taste.

Black cardamom pod Distinctively smoky aroma and a coolness similar to mint.

Black peppercorns World's most traded spice, fiery heat, citrusy, woody and floral notes.

Cardamom pod A strong, unique taste with an intensely aromatic, resinous fragrance.

Cinnamon bark Aromatic, pungent in taste, similar scent to ground cinnamon.

Cloves Highly aromatic in taste, warm and spicy, contains volatile oils.

Kashmiri chillies/chiles, dried Adds a deep-red colour, moderate spice level.

Mace, whole Stronger and more pungent than nutmeg with a savoury scent.

Nutmeg, whole Slightly sweet, warming flavour, pungent aroma.

Star anise Resembles aniseed in flavour, enhances the flavour of meat.

DRIED SEEDS

Ajwain seeds Pungent version of thyme with a pickling flavour.

Black mustard seeds Spicy, aromatic, rustic taste and smoky fragrance.

Coriander seeds Earthy, nutty flavour and slightly citrusy taste.

Cumin seeds Distinctive earthy aroma, warmly bitter flavours, draws out natural flavours.

Fennel seeds Liquorice-flavoured, sweet, aromatic, a light delicate flavour.

Fenugreek seeds Slightly bitter taste, complement seafood really well.

Onion seeds Complement fish and seafood really well, aromatic flavour, tinge of fragrance.

LEAF SPICES

Bay leaves Distinctive flavour and fragrance, with a pungent, sharp bitter taste. Extremely herbal.

Curry leaves Aromatic leaves that release a deliciously nutty aroma when fried in hot oil.

Fenugreek leaves Smoky and bitter but addictive. Strong in aroma and distinctive in flavour.

SPICE POWDERS

Cardamom powder, green A wonderful floral aroma with an enticing warm spicy-sweet flavour.

Cardamom powder, black Smokier than green cardamom powder, perfect for savoury dishes.

Cinnamon, ground A powerful, sweet and intensely fragrant spice with a warm and woody aroma.

Cloves, ground A strong, spicy flavour with a warm-hot taste that adds fragrant and floral notes.

Coriander, ground A fresh, pleasing aroma with a mild citrus flavour.

Cumin, ground An aromatic, penetrating flavour, slightly bitter, nutty taste, powerful aroma.

Curry leaf powder A distinct, delicate flavour and aroma of curry leaves.

Fenugreek powder A highly aromatic flavour, slightly souring, fragrant flavour with a bitter taste.

Garam masala A warm spice mix used to enhance the flavour in a dish. Fragrant, floral and earthy.

Ginger, ground Used as a seasoning agent to give a mild level of heat and spice.

Kashmiri chilli/chili powder Mild in taste, but still delivers good heat. Gives lovely, deep-red colour.

Mace powder Used for the bright-orange saffron-like appearance, a savoury flavour-enhancing aid.

Mango powder A fruity spice powder with a citrusy taste and sour aroma.

Methi powder Smoky flavour and a light bitter taste, with a slight level of heat.

Nutmeg, ground A slightly sweet and warming flavour, used to balance strong flavours.

Paprika, ground A woody earthy aroma that adds a mild, sweet flavour to dishes.

Star anise powder Similar to fennel seeds, stronger than anise, the liquorice flavour enhances meat.

Turmeric, ground Mildly aromatic and has scents of orange and ginger. Has a pungent, bitter flavour.

PURÉES, PASTES AND MASALAS

Most traditional Indian dishes incorporate the use of various purées, pastes and spice blends or 'masalas'. They enhance aroma, flavour, taste, texture, mouthfeel or appearance. The recipes on the following pages are the cheats that I use in my kitchen… who said good food had to be hard work!

Layering flavours When using spices, pastes and masalas, the flavours need to be layered at different times. Each recipe indicates when to do this, but it is important to cook out the fresh spices before adding the dried or ground spices to add depth of flavour to the dish.

Masala box Any traditional Indian kitchen will have a masala box, whatever size or shape (usually round), there will always be a convenient box of spices which is close to hand when cooking. In my masala box, I always keep whole cumin seeds, mustard seeds, fenugreek seeds, whole cinnamon bark, cloves, cardamom pods and whole dried chillies. Depending on the dish, these are my favourite seven spices to use to infuse in hot oil at the start of cooking sauces.

Tomato purée/paste Generally quite concentrated and can taste sharp if not cooked out properly, so make sure you mix it in well with your onions and spices when cooking.

ROTI BREADS

300 g/2 cups medium chapatti/fine ground whole-wheat flour
2 tablespoons vegetable oil
225 ml/scant 1 cup boiling water
plain/all-purpose flour, for dusting
butter, for brushing

MAKES 12

In a mixing bowl, add the flour and oil and mix well so that the flour grains are enrobed in the oil. Carefully add the boiling water and gradually mix with a fork so that the mixture starts to come together as a dough. Knead the dough for 5–6 minutes, when it will resemble a soft bread dough.

Divide the dough into 12 equal pieces. Roll each piece into a ball in your hands to smooth out any cracks, then, using the palms of your hand, flatten slightly so that you have a disc with a thick centre.

Dip the discs in the plain/all-purpose flour on both sides, then roll out to 15 cm/12 inches.

Set a heavy-bottomed frying pan/skillet over medium heat. Place the rolled out roti dough, one by one, on the hot pan and heat for no longer than 15–20 seconds. Using a fish slice, flip the roti and cook on the other side – you will see brown circular marks appear on the underneath. Flip the bread again to complete the cooking on the half-cooked side. Gently press down in the centre of the roti bread with a clean kitchen cloth, neatly scrunched up into a ball to encourage the centre of the bread to steam, rise in the middle and form air pockets.

Remove the bread from the pan and to a clean plate, brush with a little butter and repeat the process until all of the breads are cooked.

As each bread cooks, place it on top of the previously cooked bread to stop them from drying out. Serve or wrap the breads tightly in clingfilm/plastic wrap and freeze for up to 1 month.

NITISHA'S NUTTY NAANS

200 ml/¾ cup warm water
1½ teaspoons dried yeast powder
2 teaspoons caster/granulated sugar
350 g/2⅓ cups plain/all-purpose flour, plus extra for dusting
½ teaspoon salt
25 g/¼ cup chopped pistachio nuts
120 g/½ cup natural/plain yogurt (at room temperature)
3 tablespoons ghee
1 tablespoon desiccated/dried shredded coconut
melted ghee, for brushing

MAKES 5

In a measuring jug/pitcher, whisk the warm water, yeast and sugar together, cover with clingfilm/plastic wrap and rest for 10 minutes.

In a large mixing bowl, add in the flour, salt, nuts and coconut and mix well.

Mix the ghee and yogurt into the yeast mixture and whisk gently until there are no lumps.

Make a well in the centre of the flour mixture and gradually add in the liquid mixture. Using your hands, bring the mixture together to form a sticky dough. Cover the mixing bowl with clingfilm/plastic wrap and put in a warm place for 30 minutes.

Preheat the oven to 230°C (450°F) Gas 8 with a baking sheet inside.

Oil your hands and divide the mixture into 5 equal balls, roll the balls in the palms of your hands and dip into the flour of dusting. Roll out the naan breads into circles, roughly 15 cm/12 inches in diameter and 5 mm/¼ inch thick. Fold the naan breads in half, then half again to quarter-circles.

Dust with flour and using the palm of your hand, gently push the dough into slipper shapes.

Transfer the naan breads in batches to the preheated baking sheet in the preheated oven and bake for 5–6 minutes.

Brush with a little ghee and serve.

BOILED ONION PURÉE

This recipe is great to use as a creamy base in any curry sauce. It is boiled which makes it healthy and also delivers on a smooth, velvety texture. I love using this purée because it adds sweetness to dishes without having to add too much sugar.

4 large onions, sliced

MAKES 750 G/3 CUPS

Put the sliced onions in a saucepan and cover with boiling water. Bring to the boil and slowly simmer for 25–30 minutes or until the onions have completely softened and mash easily using the back of a spoon. Drain away the excess water and blitz the onions together with a stick blender to make a purée. It should last for 3–4 days refrigerated.

SEASONED OIL

Essential for the Kaali Dhal (page 96), this oil adds rich flavour and is quick to prepare.

5 tablespoons vegetable oil
5 cardamom pods
5 cloves
a 5-cm/2-inch cinnamon stick
1 teaspoon cumin seeds
1 teaspoon red chilli/chili powder
2 green chillies/chiles, slit

MAKES 400 ML/1⅔ CUPS

Heat the oil in a small pan, add the cardamom pods, cloves and cinnamon. Fry for a minute, then add the cumin seeds until sizzling. Add the remaining ingredients for 10–15 seconds. Cool before use.

HOLY TRINITY PASTE

In my opinion, this is vital to most home-cooked Gujarati-style dishes. The 'holy trinity' of green chilli/chile, garlic and ginger creates a wonderful fresh flavour. It is quite punchy, so you want to cook out all the rawness from it when it comes to layering flavours in dishes. You can quarter the quantities here for a smaller yield.

200 g/7 oz. (about 6) green chillies/chiles
200 g/7 oz. (about 40) garlic cloves
200 g/7 oz. (about 8 x 5-cm/2-inch pieces)
  fresh root ginger
50 ml/3½ tablespoons vegetable oil
1 tablespoon salt

MAKES 625 G/2½ CUPS

Blitz together the ingredients in a food processor to form a coarse paste. Refrigerate for up to 2 weeks.

CRISPY FRIED ONIONS

Adding a regal touch with a rich and deep flavour, these onions finish off any dish, but remember a little goes a long way!

1 onion, thinly sliced
1 tablespoon cornflour/cornstarch
150 ml/⅔ cup vegetable oil, for shallow-frying

MAKES 175 G/1¼ CUPS

Put the sliced onions in a bowl and sprinkle over the cornflour/cornstarch. Mix well. Heat the oil in a pan for shallow-frying, but do not allow the oil to get so hot it will burn the onions. Fry them for 5–6 minutes or until golden-brown. Remove from the oil and drain on paper towels. Set aside until required (store in an airtight container for up to 4 days).

STREET FOOD
AND SNACKS

Indian street food is one of my favourite things to eat. I absolutely love the excitement, freshness, explosive flavours, difference in textures, and snack-friendly appeal that it has. In Britain today, it is evident that there is a rise in the consumption of this style of food as a whole, however, with Indian food being the nation's favourite choice, more and more market stalls around the country are selling great-tasting Indian varieties of snacks. The same can be said in other foodie hotspots around the rest of the world. Cities with a high Asian population seem to be creating a new fashion for 'trendy food'. The rise of the food markets is encouraging more and more people to go out and embrace the street-food experience with friends and family as part of a social event.

I feel that a lot of people assume that Indian food is comprised of predominantly curry, but it is refreshing to see how many people are becoming aware of Indian foods, especially non-curry based dishes. Street food is a variety of quick, fresh and explosive-tasting food that is ready to eat, great for when you are on the go, or out and about. It is also very popular because it is usually relatively inexpensive and a great way for people to socialize over food.

Due to the vast choice and range of delicious snacks, eating throughout the day forms a large part of the Indian way of life. A way of life that is very popular with not only tourists, but locals too, from children to young couples, to the elderly. In the hustle and bustle of the world's busiest cities, food is available at all hours of the day and night at the roadside, whether it's grabbing a breakfast bite, an energizing pick-me-up lunch or an indulgent dinner, vendors with mobile stalls selling delicious handheld dishes can be found on practically every street corner in India.

With the world's second-largest population and 29 states, each with its own characteristic identity, the country is very diverse. History and geography have influenced Indian cuisine, as well as language, climate, religion, eating habits and dietary restrictions, and it is street food that shows off this diversity best. Try the Amritsari Fish Pakoras on page 20, the Smokin' Fiery Chicken Wings on page 24, or the Gujarati Dhokla Muffins on page 34 for truly delicious quick meals or snacks.

SUPERFOOD ALOO TIKKI CHAAT

I created this dish when applying for a role as an Indian development chef – it turned out to be a step too far for that particular brief, but this is the style of food that I absolutely love to eat! The term 'chaat' is used to describe the eating of several small, savoury dishes at once. The aloo tikki are quinoa-crusted sweet potato cakes that are served with chickpeas in a spiced tomato sauce known as 'channa masala'. A combination of traditional Indian heritage and modern food trends, mixing bold and exciting flavours. There are several elements to prepare here but the end result is worth it. This dish has always been a success when I have made it for friends and family. The sweet potato tikkis alone are incredibly flavoursome! (Pictured pages 18–19)

250 g/1¾ cups cooked quinoa

plain/all-purpose flour, for dusting

vegetable oil, for shallow-frying

ALOO TIKKI FILLING

300 g/scant 1½ cups mashed potatoes (Maris Piper or Yukon Gold)

200 g/scant 1 cup mashed sweet potato

1 teaspoon salt

½ teaspoon Holy Trinity Paste (page 12)

½ teaspoon ground turmeric

freshly squeezed juice of ½ lemon

2 tablespoons freshly chopped coriander/cilantro (leaves from a small bunch)

½ teaspoon Kashmiri red chilli/chili powder

¼ teaspoon baking powder

ALOO TIKKI BATTER

60 g/scant ½ cup plain/all-purpose flour

½ teaspoon ground turmeric

CHANNA MASALA

4 tablespoons vegetable oil

1 teaspoon cumin seeds

1 teaspoon ginger paste

3 large tomatoes, finely chopped (core and seeds removed)

1 green chilli/chile, sliced

1 teaspoon salt

½ teaspoon ground cumin

½ teaspoon ground coriander

½ teaspoon ground turmeric

1 teaspoon chole masala powder

240 g/1¾ cups drained canned chickpeas

1 teaspoon caster/granulated sugar

¼ teaspoon garam masala

2 tablespoons freshly chopped coriander/cilantro (leaves from a small bunch)

TO SERVE

Hariyali Chutney (page 135)

Tamarind Chutney (page 134)

coconut yogurt

fresh pomegranate seeds

pumpkin seeds

coriander/cilantro sprigs

baking sheet, lined with baking parchment

SERVES 5
(2 TIKKIS PER SERVING)

Start by making the aloo tikki filling. Add all of the ingredients to a bowl and mix well. Shape the mixture into small equal-sized patties. The mix should make 10 patties (around 50 g/2 oz. each). Place the patties on the lined baking sheet and chill in the refrigerator for 30 minutes.

While the patties are chilling, combine the flour and turmeric for the aloo tikki batter with 250 ml/ 1 cup of water and set aside.

Put the cooked quinoa on a baking sheet or shallow plate and flatten out. Gently and lightly dust 2–4 patties in the flour for dusting, coat well in the batter, then in the cooked quinoa.

Heat the oil for shallow-frying in a pan over medium heat. Shallow-fry the patties on both sides for 4–5 minutes, until the quinoa is golden-brown with a slight crisp. Drain the patties on paper towels and set aside. Continue making and frying the aloo tikkis in batches of 2–4 until cooked.

For the channa masala, heat the oil in a saucepan over medium heat, add the cumin seeds and allow to sizzle and pop. Add the ginger paste and fry until it has lost its raw aroma and the ginger begins to separate from the paste. Add the tomatoes, chilli/chile and salt and mix well for 2–3 minutes. Cover with a lid, reduce the heat and cook for 20–25 minutes or until the tomatoes have completely melted into a sauce. Stir occasionally to prevent the sauce from sticking.

Add the ground spices and mix well into the sauce. If the pan looks like it is drying out too much, add a splash of water. Add the chickpeas, sugar and 200 ml/¾ cup of water and simmer for

10 minutes. Add the garam masala and chopped coriander/cilantro, mix well, then remove from the heat and set aside (covered with a lid).

If you haven't already made the hariyali and tamarind chutneys, now is the time to do so.

The aloo tikki chaat should be prepared right before it is about to be eaten. Typically, a chaat includes lots of different ingredients, textures and also temperatures. Prepare your dishes by placing two warm patties on a plate, cover with a spoonful of the channa masala and drizzle over about 2 teaspoons each of the hariyali chutney, tamarind chutney and coconut yogurt. Sprinkle over the fresh pomegranate seeds and pumpkin seeds and garnish with a coriander/cilantro sprig.

AMRITSARI FISH PAKORAS

It does not get more 'Indian street food' than Amritsari fish pakoras! Diced cod is coated in an aromatic spiced batter and deep fried, making the perfect appetizer for any Indian meal or a snack to accompany a beer and a football match! The crispy batter complements the moist, succulent fish to create a delicious pakora. These tasty treats are traditionally found at the street-food stalls of Amritsar in Punjab, northern India, however, they are so hugely popular that they are now eaten all over the country.

500 g/1lb. 2 oz. cod loin, diced into 2.5-cm/ 1-inch cubes
plain/all-purpose flour, sifted, for dusting
vegetable oil, for deep-frying

MARINADE
2 tablespoons vegetable oil
1 tablespoon Holy Trinity Paste (page 12)
freshly squeezed juice of ½ lemon
½ teaspoon ground turmeric
½ teaspoon salt
½ teaspoon Kashmiri red chilli/chili powder

BATTER
4 tablespoons rice flour
8 tablespoons gram/ chickpea flour, sifted
1 teaspoon ajwain seeds
1 teaspoon dried chilli/ hot red pepper flakes
1 teaspoon ground turmeric
½ teaspoon baking powder
1 tablespoon freshly chopped coriander/ cilantro
180 ml/¾ cup ice-cold water
1 teaspoon salt

TO SERVE
mango powder, for sprinkling
black salt, for sprinkling
sliced chilli/chile
freshly chopped coriander/cilantro
lemon wedges

deep-fat fryer (optional)

SERVES 4–6

Rinse the diced fish under cold running water and gently pat dry.

Combine all of the ingredients for the marinade together and mix with the diced fish. Let the fish pieces marinate for a minimum of 30 minutes at room temperature and a maximum of 24 hours in the refrigerator.

Combine all of the ingredients for the batter together, then set aside for 30 minutes to allow the ingredients and flavours to all come together. It should be the consistency of double/heavy cream.

Pat the marinated fish pieces in sifted flour and shake off any excess. Dip the floured fish pieces into the batter, ensuring that the fish is fully coated in the batter, with the spices distributed evenly.

Heat the oil for deep-frying in a deep-fat fryer or large, heavy-bottomed pan to 180°C (350°F). Deep-fry the fish pieces in batches of 6–8 pieces until golden-brown and the fish is cooked through; this should take no longer than 3–4 minutes per batch. Sprinkle over a pinch of mango powder and black salt, to taste, then serve with sliced chilli/chile, chopped coriander/cilantro and lemon wedges.

BATATA VADAS

Street food is a huge part of the Indian food scene and what I find most magical about it is how so many of the dishes are completely vegetarian. This recipe showcases the beauty and versatility of the humble potato. Spiced mashed potato is coated in a gram/chickpea flour batter and deep-fried. I am extremely fond of batata vadas and have been ever since I was young. They are so easy to make and extremely delicious.

vegetable oil, for
    deep-frying
plain/all-purpose flour,
    for dusting
Tomato, Cucumber and
    Mint Raita (page 132),
    to serve

POTATO FILLING
1 kg/scant 5 cups
    mashed potatoes
    (Maris Piper or Yukon
    Gold)
2 teaspoons Holy Trinity
    Paste (page 12)
2 teaspoons salt
½ teaspoon ground
    turmeric
1 teaspoon Kashmiri
    red chilli/chili powder
2 teaspoons caster/
    granulated sugar
freshly squeezed juice
    of 1 lemon

SEASONED OIL
3 tablespoons vegetable
    oil
1 teaspoon mustard
    seeds
1 teaspoon sesame
    seeds
½ teaspoon asafoetida

BATTER
200 g/2¼ cups gram/
    chickpea flour, sifted
½ tablespoon
    cornflour/cornstarch
1 teaspoon ground
    turmeric
1 teaspoon salt

*baking sheet, lined with
baking parchment
deep-fat fryer (optional)*

SERVES 4–6

Combine all of the ingredients for the potato filling together and mix well.

For the seasoned oil, heat the oil in a small saucepan over medium heat, add the mustard seeds and allow to sizzle and crackle. Add the sesame seeds, shake around in the pan, then add the asafoetida and stir with a spatula or wooden spoon for 10 seconds. Remove the saucepan from the heat.

Pour the hot seasoned oil into the filling mixture and mix well again.

Shape the mixture into golf ball-sized pieces, place on the lined baking sheet and put in the refrigerator to chill.

Mix all of the ingredients for the batter together with 230 ml/scant 1 cup of water. Set aside.

Heat the oil for deep-frying in a deep-fat fryer or large, heavy-bottomed pan to 180°C (350°F). Gently roll the balls around in the flour for dusting (in batches of 4–5) and then dip into the batter.

Place the battered balls into the hot oil and deep-fry until they become golden-brown; this should take 4–5 minutes. Drain on paper towels. Repeat with the rest of the balls.

Serve the batata vadas with tomato, cucumber and mint raita and enjoy!

SMOKIN' FIERY CHICKEN WINGS

Wings are my favourite cut of chicken – they are moist, tender and oh, so flavoursome! They are also incredibly versatile which is why they work so well with intense flavours such as smoky paprika and hot spices. Even though it's a very simple recipe, I decided to include it in the book because it has never let me down and always impresses my guests. Charring the wings before baking means they really are smokin'!

2 tablespoons vegetable oil
1 teaspoon salt
3 teaspoons Holy Trinity Paste (page 12)
freshly squeezed juice of 1 lemon
1 teaspoon ground cumin
1 teaspoon ground coriander
1 teaspoon ground turmeric
1 teaspoon paprika
½ teaspoon dried chilli/hot red pepper flakes
½ teaspoon tandoori masala

2 tablespoons natural/plain yogurt
1 teaspoon Kashmiri red chilli/chili powder
1 teaspoon dried fenugreek leaves
1 kg/2¼ lbs. chicken wings

TO SERVE
dipping sauce or chutney of your choosing
lime wedges

SERVES 4

In a large mixing bowl, combine all of the ingredients apart from the chicken wings. Mix well until the mixture is smooth, then add in the chicken wings and mix to coat. Allow the wings to marinate overnight in the refrigerator, if possible, or for a minimum of 30 minutes at room temperature.

Preheat the oven to 180°C (350°F) Gas 4.

Heat a griddle pan until smoking (if you don't have a griddle pan you can use a heavy-bottomed frying pan/skillet). Seal the wings in the hot pan to create a smoky, charred flavour on the skin. Transfer the wings to a large baking sheet and bake in the preheated oven for 25 minutes.

Serve as a snack or appetizer with a dipping sauce or chutney and a squeeze of lime for a final flourish of zestiness.

SAMOSA CHAAT

Samosas are probably the most popular and widely recognized Indian snack. On their own, they showcase the versatility of the humble potato as a filling, but when eaten as a chaat, the snack is completely transformed and becomes an explosion of flavours. The addition of the channa masala, chutneys, yogurt, red onion and crispy sev adds a completely different dimension to the dish. Each mouthful is an adventure! (Pictured pages 28–29)

SAMOSA FILLING
- 4 tablespoons vegetable oil
- 1 teaspoon cumin seeds
- 1½ teaspoons coriander seeds, crushed
- ½ teaspoon finely chopped green chilli/chile
- 1 teaspoon grated fresh root ginger
- 350 g/12 oz. boiled, crushed potatoes (Maris Piper or Yukon Gold, boiled and broken with hands; not mashed)
- 1 teaspoon salt
- ½ teaspoon Kashmiri red chilli/chili powder
- 75 g/scant ½ cup frozen peas, defrosted
- 1 tablespoon freshly chopped coriander/cilantro
- vegetable oil, for deep-frying

PASTRY
- 200 g/1⅔ cups plain/all-purpose flour
- ½ teaspoon ajwain seeds
- ½ teaspoon salt
- 2 tablespoons melted ghee
- 60 ml/¼ cup hot water (not boiling)

TO SERVE
- Channa Masala (page 16)
- Hariyali Chutney (page 135)
- Tamarind Chutney (page 134)
- natural/plain yogurt
- red onion, finely chopped
- sev (deep-fried thin noodles made from gram/chickpea flour paste)
- coriander/cilantro sprigs

deep-fat fryer (optional)

SERVES 4
(4 MINI SAMOSAS PER SERVING)

Start by making the samosas. It is best to make the filling first, as you can let it cool while you make the pastry. Heat the vegetable oil in a pan over medium heat. Add the cumin seeds and fry until they start to sizzle and crackle, then add the crushed coriander seeds and fry in the cumin seed oil for 15 seconds. Add the green chilli/chile and ginger and fry for about 20 seconds until the ginger fibres all start to separate from one another in the pan. Add the crushed potatoes, salt and red chilli/chili powder and stir well in the oil until all of the potato is well-coated. Cook until the potatoes are fully warmed through, then add the peas and chopped coriander/cilantro and mix well.

Transfer the filling to a baking sheet or large plate, spread out and allow to cool.

To make the pastry, put the flour, ajwain seeds and salt in a bowl and mix. Pour in the melted ghee and gently rub in using your fingertips. When the ghee is well distributed in the flour, pour in the hot water, a little at a time, and bring the mixture together to form a dough. Knead and work the dough until it is smooth with no visible cracks – it should be the same texture as bread dough. Cover the dough with some greased clingfilm/plastic wrap and set aside.

Once the filling has cooled completely, make the pastry sheets for each individual samosa. Divide the dough into eight even balls and roll out to 12.5-cm/5-inch circles. Cut each circle in half creating 16 equal semi-circles.

Build the samosas one by one, by making a cone shape with a semi-circle of pastry; bring one side to overlap with the other side of the pastry and seal the edge together with a little bit of water. Gently hold the cone in one hand (do not allow the cone to close while it is empty as the pastry may stick together) and pinch the tip to seal (this will prevent it from letting in oil when deep-frying). Using a teaspoon, spoon a little of the filling into the pastry cone, then use the spoon as an aid to gently push in the filling. Do not over-fill; leave a lip of pastry (around 1 cm/⅜ inch). Using your fingertips, brush a little water around the inner exposed part of the pastry and seal by pressing the two sides together to form a sealed triangle. Repeat the process to create 16 samosas.

Heat the oil for deep-frying in a deep- fat fryer or large, heavy-bottomed pan to 180°C (350°F). Deep-fry the samosas, in batches of 4–5, until golden-brown; this should take 5–6 minutes. Drain on paper towels and set aside until required.

If you haven't already made the hariyali and tamarind chutneys, now is the time to do so.

A chaat should be prepared right before it is about to be eaten. Place 4 warm mini samosas on a plate, cover with a spoonful of the channa masala and drizzle over about 2 teaspoons each of the hariyali chutney, tamarind chutney and natural/plain yogurt. Sprinkle over some red onion, sev and coriander/cilantro sprigs, and serve.

GRILLED LAMB CHOPS

If I could, I would eat lamb chops everyday. Every single day in fact. Lamb is my favourite meat, and lamb chops particularly are my most loved cut. Personally, I love the 'gamey' flavour and the succulent fat running through the meat. My earliest memories of eating spicy grilled lamb chops are based around meals in the numerous 'Desi Pubs' we have here in the Black Country. The term 'Desi Pub', is what we use for a pub where the landlord is of an Indian (mainly Punjabi), heritage. Whilst the Pubs inherently still maintain and boast their British elements of beers, ales and pub games, the main attraction is certainly the food! The grilled meats found in the hundreds of Black Country Desi Pubs definitely pay a true homage to the traditional Tandoori cafes and restaurants on the bustling streets of Punjab. Here is my recipe for Indian Grilled Lamb Chops… simple but sumptuously satisfying…

2 teaspoons cumin
    seeds
4 tablespoons natural/
    plain yogurt
1 teaspoon salt
5 garlic cloves
a 5-cm/2-inch piece of
    fresh root ginger
4 green chillies/chiles
1 red chilli/chile
1 teaspoon ground
    turmeric
1 teaspoon garam
    masala
5 fresh mint leaves,
    plus extra to garnish
freshly squeezed juice
    of ½ lemon
12 lamb chops
vegetable oil, for frying

SERVES 4

Toast the cumin seeds in a dry frying pan/skillet over low–medium heat until they become dark in colour and give off a fragrant aroma. Put all of the ingredients (including the toasted cumin seeds, but not the lamb chops) in a food processor and blitz until everything comes together to form a coarse chunky paste.

Rub the paste all over the lamb chops, wearing gloves if needed. Allow the chops to marinate for 24 hours in the refrigerator if possible, or for at least 30 minutes at room temperature.

Preheat the grill/broiler to high.

Heat a little oil in a frying pan/skillet over medium heat and seal the chops on both sides for 1 minute. Transfer to a baking sheet and put under the preheated grill/boiler. Grill/broil the chops for 5 minutes on each side for medium-rare. If you want them more well-done, then leave them under the grill/broiler for a little longer.

Sprinkle the chops with mint leaves and serve straight away to prevent them from drying out.

PULLED TANDOORI LAMB KATHI ROLL

4 tablespoons vegetable oil, plus extra for shallow-frying
1 teaspoon cumin seeds
1 tablespoon diced fresh root ginger
½ red onion, sliced
½ teaspoon salt
½ teaspoon Holy Trinity Paste (page 12)
½ teaspoon ground cumin
½ teaspoon ground coriander
½ teaspoon ground turmeric
2 tomatoes, chopped (core and seeds removed)
1 tablespoon tomato purée/paste
250 g/9 oz. pulled cooked lamb meat (or any other leftover meat)
Tomato, Cucumber and Mint Raita (page 130), to serve

EGG-FRIED WRAPS
4 eggs
½ teaspoon ground turmeric
4 roti breads (tortilla wraps work just as well)

SERVES 4

Most world cuisines have their own version of a wrap; the Mexicans have burritos, the Japanese have sushi rolls, the Greeks have souvlaki pitta wraps and the Indians have, what I think is by far the most delicious wrap… the ingenious kathi roll; a roti bread dipped in whisked egg, spread with any filling of your choice and then rolled. An egg-fried wrap! Any vegetable, meat or fish filling goes well with the soft fried casing. My favourite filling is this Tandoori pulled lamb because it's both delicious and a great way to use up leftover lamb meat the day after a roast.

To make the filling, heat the vegetable oil in a heavy-bottomed saucepan over medium heat and fry the cumin seeds until they sizzle and pop. Add the ginger and fry until it browns lightly. Add the onion and salt and fry gently until the onion softens. Next, fry the holy trinity paste until it has completely lost its raw aroma. Add all of the ground spices and fry gently to cook them out. If the pan is drying out slightly, you can add a splash of water.

Next, add the tomatoes, mix well, reduce the heat slightly and cover with a lid. Simmer for 15 minutes, stirring every 5 minutes and allowing the tomatoes to gently melt down and form a sauce. Add the tomato purée/paste, stir and add 200 ml/¾ cup of water and mix well. Add the pulled cooked lamb meat (or whatever meat you would like to use), mix well and simmer for a further 10 minutes. The sauce should have thickened with the lamb meat to form a filling. Set aside until required.

The kathi rolls are best eaten when prepared at the very last minute, so only fry as many wraps as required.

To make the egg-fried wraps, whisk together the eggs and turmeric, then pour onto a large, shallow plate. Dip a roti bread into the mixture so that it is well-coated on both sides with the egg. Shallow-fry on both sides until the egg is cooked. Repeat for the remaining wraps.

Assemble the kathi wraps by first spooning on the lamb mixture and then drizzling over a little raita. Wrap each kathi roll tightly and leave one end open so that you can see the filling inside.

Serve immediately with the remaining raita alongside.

DHOKLA MUFFINS

50 g/¼ cup caster/
granulated sugar

BATTER
190 g/1¼ cups semolina
25 g/¼ cup gram/
chickpea flour
230 g/generous 1 cup
natural/plain yogurt
½ teaspoon finely
grated garlic
1 teaspoon finely grated
fresh root ginger
1 teaspoon chopped
green chilli/chile
1 teaspoon caster/
granulated sugar
1 teaspoon salt
150 ml/⅔ cup warm
water
1½ teaspoons fruit salt

SEASONED OIL
3 tablespoons vegetable
oil
1 teaspoon each of
mustard seeds and
sesame seeds

TO SERVE
freshly chopped
coriander/cilantro
unsweetened
desiccated/dried
shredded coconut
Hariyali or Coconut
Chutney (page 135)

steamer (optional)
8 muffin moulds, greased
and lined with baking
parchment

SERVES 4

The dhokla is a very traditional Gujarati snack, and being a Gujarati girl myself, I thought it necessary to include a recipe for it in my book because I hold it very close to my heart. I have served dhokla to lots of people who have never heard of it before, all of whom have been impressed. They are savoury steamed muffins made from gram/chickpea flour. Because the savoury, light, fluffy cake is steamed, it is healthy and nutritious as well as packing a flavour punch.

Combine all of the ingredients for the batter together apart from the fruit salt. Cover the batter and leave for 10 minutes to rest and ferment.

Meanwhile, set up your steamer. If you do not have a steamer, you can pour boiling water into a large saucepan and insert a stand for the moulds to sit on (the moulds should not touch the water directly). At this point you need to ensure that the steamer is absolutely ready, because once you put the fruit salt into the fermented batter, you need to cook the muffins straight away for the best texture. Set the muffin moulds out ready for use. If you do not have metal muffin moulds, you can also use ramekins.

Once you are all set up, quickly add the fruit salt and 2 teaspoons of water to the batter and mix well. Quickly and evenly distribute the batter between the moulds. Put them into the steamer with a lid on and steam for 10–12 minutes.

You can check whether the muffins are ready or not by poking the centre with a clean knife; if the knife comes out clean, then the muffins are fully cooked. They should be light and spongy. Remove the muffins from the steamer and set aside to cool.

While they are cooling, prepare a sugared water by heating the sugar and 200 ml/¾ cup of water together in a pan until the sugar completely dissolves. Set the pan aside and leave to cool slightly.

Take the muffins out of the moulds and put on a wire rack, gently prick with a cocktail stick/toothpick and pour a little of the sugared water over each muffin, no more than a tablespoonful on each.

Next, make the seasoned oil. Heat the oil in a frying pan/skillet over medium heat, add the mustard seeds and allow to sizzle and pop. Add the sesame seeds, mix well for 10 seconds and remove from the heat. Spoon a little of the oil and seed mix onto each muffin. Garnish with the chopped coriander/cilantro and coconut.

Serve warm or cold, with either the hariyali or coconut chutney.

MASALA DHAL VADAS

Dhal vadas make a great snack; they are made from a spiced lentil mixture that is deep-fried to form fritters. This recipe showcases just how versatile lentils are. Lentils have a wonderful texture, and the beauty of these fritters is that once deep-fried, the outer layer is crispy and crunchy while the inner part is soft and moreish. Like most street food, this recipe is vegetarian and is great for serving at dinner parties as an appetizer.

200 g/1 cup dried split channa dhal soaked in 600 ml/2½ cups water for 6 hours (this should yield a total of 350 g/2¼ cups)
½ teaspoon salt
1 teaspoon grated fresh root ginger
1 teaspoon chopped green chilli/chile
100 g/scant ½ cup mashed potatoes (Maris Piper or Yukon Gold)
¼ teaspoon asafoetida
½ teaspoon Kashmiri red chilli/chili powder
½ teaspoon ground turmeric
2 tablespoons freshly chopped coriander/cilantro
¼ onion, finely chopped
vegetable oil, for deep-frying and greasing
chutney of your choice, to serve (Coconut Chutney, page 135, works well to mellow the heat of the dish)

deep-fat fryer (optional)

SERVES 4
(MAKES 16 VADAS)

Remove 2 tablespoons of the soaked channa dhal and set aside until required. Using a food processor, blitz together the remaining channa dhal until all of the lentils have been coarsely chopped.

Combine all of the ingredients, including the dhal, in a mixing bowl and mix well to form a fritter batter. Grease your hands with a little oil and roll into 16 fritters about 30 g/1 oz. each. I shape them into balls to start with and then flatten them with the palm of my hands so that they look like patties that are slightly thicker in the middle and thinner on the edges.

Heat the oil for deep-frying in a deep-fat fryer or large, heavy-bottomed pan to 180°C (350°F). Deep-fry the fritters in batches in the hot oil until golden-brown; this should take 5–6 minutes. (The fritters should be crunchy on the outside and soft in the inside.) Drain and serve warm with chutney.

MALAI, TANDOORI AND HARIYALI CHICKEN TIKKA KEBABS/KABOBS

This dish makes a great appetizer or light lunch. With three different, colourful marinades to choose from, it looks wonderful when presented at the table as part of a feast. This dish is also rather special to me as it represents the flag of India in a tasty way. The white Malai marinade is creamy, fragrant and has a rich flavour that is mildly spiced. The orange Tandoori marinade is full of spice and citrus notes. The green Hariyali marinade has a fresh spice from green chillies/chiles, citrus from lime and herbiness from the mint and coriander/cilantro. (Pictured pages 40–41)

900 g/2 lb. chicken breast, cut into 4-cm/1½-inch cubes

MALAI MARINADE
4 tablespoons Boiled Onion Purée (page 12)
1 teaspoon garlic purée
1 teaspoon ginger purée
1 teaspoon cardamom powder
½ teaspoon crushed black pepper
1½ teaspoons salt
1 teaspoon dried fenugreek leaves
2 tablespoons vegetable oil
2 tablespoons natural/plain yogurt
2 tablespoons single/light cream
½ teaspoon fennel powder

TANDOORI MARINADE
1 teaspoon Holy Trinity Paste (page 12)
2 tablespoons natural/plain yogurt
1 teaspoon ground turmeric
2 teaspoons paprika
2 teaspoons salt
1 teaspoon ground cumin
1 teaspoon ground coriander
1 tablespoon vegetable oil
1 teaspoon cumin seeds
freshly squeezed juice of ½ lemon
1 tablespoon freshly chopped coriander/cilantro
1 teaspoon dried chilli/hot red pepper flakes

1 teaspoon dried fenugreek leaves
1 tablespoon gram/chickpea flour, lightly toasted in a frying pan/skillet until golden-brown
1 tablespoon Boiled Onion Purée (page 12)

HARIYALI MARINADE
a small bunch of mint, leaves only
a small bunch of coriander/cilantro, leaves and stalks
2 green chillies/chiles
3 garlic cloves
a 2.5-cm/1-inch squared piece of fresh root ginger
freshly squeezed juice of 1 lime

2 tablespoons Boiled Onion Purée (page 12)
1 teaspoon salt
2 tablespoons natural/plain yogurt
1 teaspoon ground cumin
1 teaspoon ground coriander
1 tablespoon gram/chickpea flour

TO SERVE
naan bread
mint leaves
Tomato, Cucumber and Mint Raita (page 130)
lime wedges

skewers

SERVES 6

Combine all of the ingredients for the malai marinade in a bowl and mix well. Repeat the same process in a separate bowl for the tandoori marinade. To make the hariyali marinade, it is best to use a food processor to blitz all of the ingredients together.

I use around 80 g/3 oz. of each marinade to 300 g/10½ oz. diced chicken. However, you can increase or decrease the amount of marinade on your chicken to your own taste. (To check the flavour of any of the three marinades, you can either roast or fry one piece of chicken, cook through and taste, then adjust as required.)

Divide the chicken into three portions and mix one portion of chicken into each of the marinades. For best results, allow each type of chicken to marinate overnight in the refrigerator or for a minimum of 30 minutes at room temperature.

Preheat the oven to 180°C (350°F) Gas 4.

Thread the marinated chicken pieces onto skewers. I prefer to prepare the skewers by keeping each marinated variety separate while cooking and then taking the chicken off the skewers just before serving. If you are making this dish for a dinner party, it is also a nice idea to place two pieces of each variety onto one skewer, so that each serving has a portion of each chicken.

In order to replicate the tandoor/clay oven flavour, sear each kebab/kabob on all sides in a smoking-hot griddle pan until there are visible charred marks all over the meat. Transfer to a baking sheet and roast the kebabs/kabobs in the preheated oven for 15 minutes until the chicken is cooked through.

Serve while still warm with naan bread, mint leaves, raita and lime wedges to squeeze over.

ALL ABOUT CURRY

Curries are dishes that I hold very close to my heart. I truly believe that I have been brought up on the world's best curries cooked by my mother and grandmother. The beauty of curry is that nothing defines what makes a good curry as recipes vary by region, religion, culture, climate, and between families. Curry houses have extensive menus, which have a vast array of dishes ranging from mild, nutty kormas, to stir-fried-style jalfrezis and fiery vindaloos. An increasing number of diners have developed an appetite for hot and spicy flavours, which in turn has boosted demand for authentic Indian dishes.

One of the key things I explain when teaching my curry masterclasses is that the beauty of the curry is just as much about the cooking process as it is about the ingredients. You can use the most beautiful, organic ingredients in the world, but if you are not treating your ingredients with the respect that they deserve and cooking with integrity, you are setting yourself up to fail. Almost every good curry starts off with a frying process, and whether that is frying out whole spices or onions first, the temperature of the pan is essential. Cooking in cold to warm oil will not allow your ingredients to release their natural oils.

If your curry involves a 'tarka' (tempered spice) stage, it is important to get the oil nice and hot. Infuse the whole spices first until you smell their aromas, then add the seeds, being careful not to burn them as this will create an undesired pungent flavour. You know when the tarka is ready as the seeds will start to dance around in the pan, crackling and sizzling.

The cooking of onion is the most important part of any curry sauce process. The darker and more caramelized the onion, the more intense the sauce; the lighter and more gently cooked the onion, the lighter and creamier the sauce.

Most curry sauces are tomato-based. As a cheat in my curry sauces, rather than using a large amount of tomatoes and cooking them for a long time to enhance the flavour, I use the addition of tomato purée/paste. This reduces the cooking time and delivers a rich flavour, depth, colour and body to the sauce. Some curries, such as kormas, do not use tomatoes but rely heavily upon the onions and the finishing agents such as cream and yogurt.

What constitutes a good curry is a matter of personal taste, but as long as your ingredients lend themselves to the dish well and have been cooked in the right way it will work. Don't be fooled by what you see in curry houses and on supermarket shelves, not all sauces have to be thick in consistency. In fact, in the north-west of India in Gujarat, the curries sauces are generally very thin and broth-like.

KERALAN PRAWN CURRY

500 g/1 lb. 2 oz. fresh
   raw king prawns/
   jumbo shrimp (heads
   and shells left on)
3 tablespoons vegetable
   oil, plus extra for frying
freshly squeezed juice
   of ½ lemon
1 teaspoon Holy Trinity
   Paste (page 12)
1 teaspoon ground
   turmeric
1 teaspoon salt

CURRY SAUCE
6 tablespoons vegetable
   oil
2 cloves
1 teaspoon cumin seeds
1 teaspoon mustard
   seeds
1 tablespoon each of
   finely diced fresh
   ginger and garlic
30 fresh curry leaves
1 large onion, finely
   chopped
2 teaspoons salt
1 teaspoon thinly sliced
   green chilli/chile
1 teaspoon each of
   ground turmeric,
   cumin, coriander
   and paprika
2 tablespoons tomato
   purée/paste
1 tablespoon palm
   sugar/jaggery
a 400-ml/14-oz. can
   coconut milk
2 teaspoons garam
   masala
1 tablespoon freshly
   chopped coriander/
   cilantro

SERVES 4

The essence of Keralan cuisine is fundamentally a result of the fertile land, and the ingredients produced there. From the sweet coconut, pungent mustard seeds to the aromatic curry leaves, the cuisine is simply marvellous. In my opinion, those key Keralan flavours are perfectly paired with plump prawns… the plumper the better!

Prepare the prawns/shrimp by removing the eyes and the black vein that runs down the back of its spine. Rinse gently and leave to drain.

Combine the vegetable oil, lemon juice, holy trinity paste, ground turmeric and salt to make the marinade for the prawns/shrimp and pour it over them. Mix well and refrigerate for a minimum of 1 hour to marinate.

To make the curry sauce, heat the oil in a heavy-bottomed wok over medium heat until hot. Add the cloves and cumin and mustard seeds and allow them to sizzle and pop. Add the ginger and garlic and fry for 1 minute until slightly golden. Add the curry leaves and let them sizzle for 10 seconds, being cautious as the oil will spit as soon as the curry leaves go into the wok. Add the onion, salt and green chilli/chile and fry until the onion is softened and golden-brown. Covering the wok with a lid will help the onion cook quicker.

Add depth to this sauce by adding in the ground turmeric, cumin, coriander and paprika. Mix them well into the mixture and gently fry the spices for 2 minutes, stirring well. Add a splash of water to stop the wok from drying out too much and burning. When the spices have cooked out, add the tomato purée/paste, mix well and fry for a further 5 minutes, adding another splash of water if the wok is becoming too dry.

Add the palm sugar/jaggery and gently simmer for 2 minutes. Next, pour in the coconut milk, mix well and simmer for a good 5 minutes to ensure all of the flavours are becoming well infused. Once the coconut milk has warmed through, add 300 ml/1¼ cups of water to loosen the sauce. Leave to simmer over low heat for 2 minutes.

Heat the oil for frying in a frying pan/skillet until smoking. One by one, add the prawns/shrimp into the pan going around in a circle, so that when all of the prawns/shrimp have been placed in the pan, you can then turn them over in the order they were added once they start to turn pink.

Add the garam masala to the curry sauce in the wok and stir in. Add the pan-fried prawns/shrimp to the sauce and mix in well. Simmer for a good 3–4 minutes until they are well cooked through. Add the coriander/cilantro, then remove from the heat. This curry is best eaten with basmati rice or naan bread.

MUMMY JI'S CHICKEN CURRY

In my opinion this is the ultimate chicken curry. It is based on the one that I grew up eating and it is like no chicken curry that you will have tried! Call me biased, but I believe my mum's chicken curry to be by far the best. Not every curry sauce has to be rich and thick and this recipe proves it. The success of the dish lies in cooking the chicken on the bone, which not only keeps the meat moist, but also adds a depth of broth-like flavour to the sauce. The sauce itself is a relatively thin gravy which has different layers of flavour, created using a variety of spices at different stages of the cooking process.

1.5 kg/3 lb. 5 oz. chicken on the bone, portioned into pieces
boiled rice, to serve

MARINADE
2 tablespoons vegetable oil
freshly squeezed juice of ½ lemon
2 tablespoons natural/plain yogurt
3 teaspoons Holy Trinity Paste (page 12)
1 teaspoon Kashmiri chilli/chili powder
1½ teaspoons ground turmeric
1½ teaspoons ground cumin
1½ teaspoons ground coriander
1½ teaspoons salt
1 teaspoon garam masala

CURRY SAUCE
5 tablespoons vegetable oil
a 5-cm/2-inch cinnamon stick
5 cloves
2 star anise
3 fresh bay leaves
a 2.5-cm/1-inch squared piece of fresh root ginger, thinly sliced
3 garlic cloves, roughly chopped
2½ large onions, finely chopped
1 teaspoon salt
6 large tomatoes, chopped (core and seeds removed)
1 teaspoon garam masala
2 tablespoons freshly chopped coriander/cilantro (leaves from a small bunch)

SERVES 6

Combine all of the ingredients for the marinade and mix together. Stir in the chicken and allow to marinate overnight in the refrigerator or for a minimum of 30 minutes at room temperature.

To make the curry sauce, heat the vegetable oil in a deep, heavy-bottomed pan over medium heat, add the cinnamon stick, cloves and star anise and fry for 1 minute to allow the aromatic oils of the spices to be released into the oil. Add the bay leaves, ginger and garlic and move around in the pan for 1 minute until the garlic and ginger are golden-brown.

Add the onions and salt and fry until completely softened and golden-brown; about 25–30 minutes. (Using a lid will help to cook the onions quicker.)

Add the tomatoes and cook until they have softened and melted and the ingredients are coming together to form a sauce base.

Next, add the marinated chicken pieces, mixing really well in the pan and sealing them all over. Once sealed, pour in 500 ml/2 cups of water, mix well, place the lid back on and let the curry simmer for 20–25 minutes until the chicken is cooked and the liquid has reduced to give a sauce-like consistency. Add the garam masala and chopped coriander/cilantro and serve with rice.

UNCLE RAMBO'S GRAND GOAT CURRY

This delicacy came to my attention one cold November evening; my cousins and I had been out the night before to celebrate my birthday and we were feeling a little rough the next day. My uncle decided to invite the family over the next evening for a meal, and the memory of what I ate that night will stay with me forever. With a family as large and as close as mine, I'm used to great food, however, this curry really blew me away. I was in complete and utter shock that my uncle, who was always up for a joke and a laugh with us, was capable of producing such a deliciously intense and meaty dish. When I asked him how he made it, he simply shrugged his shoulders, took a swig of his beer and replied, 'I just added stuff to the pan when the time was right,' and that was it... the secret ingredient is time! Be patient with this curry, it's almost a stew and the goat requires a good few hours to slowly cook away with the spices until tender. Uncle Rambo and I have spent a few afternoons together recently, him cooking away while I jot down what he's doing, and here you have it, our perfect goat curry. Thank you, Uncle! (Pictured page 50)

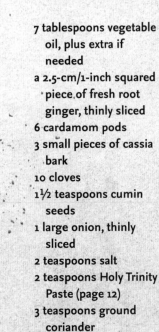

7 tablespoons vegetable oil, plus extra if needed

a 2.5-cm/1-inch squared piece of fresh root ginger, thinly sliced

6 cardamom pods

3 small pieces of cassia bark

10 cloves

1½ teaspoons cumin seeds

1 large onion, thinly sliced

2 teaspoons salt

2 teaspoons Holy Trinity Paste (page 12)

3 teaspoons ground coriander

1½ teaspoons ground cumin

½ teaspoon ground turmeric

1 kg/2¼ lbs. goat on the bone, portioned into pieces (leg or shoulder both work well for this recipe)

3 large tomatoes, chopped (core and seeds removed)

2 tablespoons tomato purée/paste

1 teaspoon garam masala

2 tablespoons freshly chopped coriander/cilantro (leaves from a small bunch)

boiled rice, to serve

SERVES 5

Heat the vegetable oil in a heavy-bottomed saucepan over medium heat, add the slices of ginger and fry until they become golden-brown. Add the aromatic spices; the cardamom pods, cassia bark and cloves, and fry for 1 minute in the hot oil to release the natural oils and aromas. Sprinkle in the cumin seeds and fry until the seeds sizzle and pop, then add the onion and salt and fry until the onion browns and softens. This should take 25–30 minutes – be patient and allow the onion to brown gently. If the pan starts to dry out, add a drizzle of oil.

Once the onion has softened, add the holy trinity paste and fry out for 5 minutes until the raw aroma has been cooked off. Add the ground coriander, cumin and turmeric and fry for 2–3 minutes. If the pan starts to dry out, add a drizzle of oil.

Once the spices have cooked out, the base of the sauce has been formed. Add the diced goat and mix to coat really well. Allow the meat to seal all over in the pan for 30 minutes, stirring occasionally. (After 30 minutes, the goat meat should start to release its natural juices.)

Add the tomatoes and mix really well, then allow the tomatoes to melt in the saucepan for 30 minutes.

Once the tomatoes have completely melted in with the goat meat, add 500 ml/2 cups of water, cover with a lid and allow to simmer over medium heat for 30 minutes.

Repeat the process of adding water and simmering five times so that the total stewing time is 3 hours (adding more water – up to 3 litres/quarts – if you need to, to reach the desired sauce consistency and ensuring the goat meat is tender and falling off the bone). For this curry, a thick sauce lends itself well to the tender goat meat so it should be similar to double/heavy cream.

The goat meat does not require a marinade in this recipe because I like the natural meaty richness of the goat meat to come through quite strongly. Not having a marinating stage does save time, but if you feel that the total cooking time is too long, you can always use a pressure cooker to cook the goat until it is tender.

Once the goat meat is cooked, tender and succulent, add the tomato purée/paste, mix well and allow the curry to simmer for 2–3 minutes. You don't need to cook the tomato purée/paste out for too long in this recipe, as the rich sauce requires a fresh tangy note from the purée/paste. Sprinkle in the garam masala and freshly chopped coriander/cilantro, mix well, then serve with boiled rice.

GOAN PORK VINDALOO

Here in the UK, when one hears 'Vindaloo', I imagine they are immediately transported to a heaving curry house on a Friday night where a group of lairy lads have dared one another to try and attempt the spiciest dish on the menu for a laugh. What many don't realize however, is just how deep rooted in colonial history the Vindaloo dish actually is! The curry as we know it today is actually based on the Portuguese dish *carne de vinha d'alhos* (meat in wine and garlic). And *carne de vinha d'alhos* came to fruition mainly as a way for the Portuguese sailors to preserve their meat for long periods at a time when sailing the seas in a quest to discover new land. Upon arriving at the golden Goan shores, the dish was soon adapted by the local Goan cooks who substituted the wine for palm vinegar and a generous addition of spices in abundance. Another incredible story of how food has journeyed across the globe! (Pictured page 51)

1.5 kg/3 lb. 5 oz. pork
  shoulder, diced
2 tablespoons vegetable
  oil, for sealing

MARINADE
10 dried Kashmiri
  chillies/chiles
1½ teaspoons cumin
  seeds
a 1.5-cm/½-inch piece
  of cassia bark
5 cloves
1 teaspoon coriander
  seeds
1 teaspoon black
  peppercorns
1 teaspoon ground
  turmeric
1 teaspoon salt
3 garlic cloves
3 tablespoons malt
  vinegar
4 tablespoons vegetable
  oil

CURRY SAUCE
5 tablespoons vegetable
  oil
1 teaspoon mustard
  seeds
1 teaspoon cumin seeds
a 2.5-cm/1-inch squared
  piece of fresh root
  ginger, thinly sliced
5 green chillies/chiles,
  slit
2 garlic cloves, thinly
  sliced
2 large onions, finely
  chopped
1 teaspoon salt
1 teaspoon ground
  cumin
1 teaspoon ground
  coriander
1 teaspoon paprika
1 teaspoon ground
  turmeric

1 teaspoon dried chilli/
  hot red pepper flakes
3 tablespoons tomato
  purée/paste
4 large tomatoes,
  chopped (core and
  seeds removed)
1 tablespoon palm
  sugar/jaggery
1 tablespoon malt
  vinegar

TO SERVE
thinly sliced red onion
boiled rice or naan
  bread (Nitisha's Nutty
  Naans, page 11)

SERVES 6

Start by making the marinade. In a frying pan/skillet, toast the Kashmiri chillies/chiles, cumin seeds, cassia bark, cloves, coriander seeds and black peppercorns over low–medium heat. Remove from the heat when the spices start to smell aromatic. Grind the spices to a powder using a pestle and mortar or a spice or coffee grinder.

Add the remaining ingredients for the marinade to a mini food processor along with the spice blend. If you do not have a mini food processor, use a pestle and mortar. Blend all of the ingredients together to form a smooth paste.

Place the diced pork in a mixing bowl and add the marinade paste. Mix well so that the pork is coated all over. If you are using your hands, make sure you wear some gloves and thoroughly wash your hands afterwards. Allow the pork to marinate for a minimum of 2 hours or up to 24 hours in the refrigerator for a more intense flavour.

Once the meat has been marinated, heat the 2 tablespoons of oil for sealing in a heavy-bottomed pan until the oil is smoking. Add the pork in batches and seal all over; do not overcrowd the pan as you will cool down the temperature of the pan. When all of the pork is sealed, transfer to a baking sheet and set aside.

Add a splash of water to deglaze the pan and loosen up all of the meat juices. Drain the flavoured water into a measuring jug/cup and set aside as you will need it at a later stage.

For the curry sauce, heat the oil in the pan, add the mustard seeds and cook until they pop, then add the cumin seeds. When the cumin seeds have crackled, add the ginger, chillies/chiles and garlic and stir in the hot oil for 1 minute. Add the onions and salt and stir well over high heat to brown the onions. Once the onions have browned, reduce the heat and cover with a lid. Gently fry the onions until they have softened and browned. This should take 25–30 minutes, but the caramelized flavour will be worth it.

Once the onions have softened, add the ground cumin, coriander, paprika, turmeric and dried chilli/hot red pepper flakes. Fry the spices for 1 minute to lose their raw aroma.

Add the tomato purée/paste and fry for 2 minutes to cook away the sour acidic notes. Loosen the sauce base by adding the reserved deglazing water.

Gently add the pork back into the pan and mix well. Pour in any juices that you may have left in the bottom of the sheet. Add 500 ml/2 cups of water, stir well, cover with a lid and simmer over low heat for 30 minutes.

Add the tomatoes, mix well and cook for a further 30 minutes over low heat with the lid on, stirring occasionally. When the tomatoes have nicely melted into the liquid to form a sauce, your curry is almost ready. Add the sugar and vinegar and cook for a further 5 minutes to let all of the flavours mingle.

Remove from the heat, garnish with red onion and serve with either rice or naan bread.

PANEER KADHAI

This recipe is a north Indian, Punjabi-style dish that is an absolute winner for vegetarians. Paneer is an Indian set cheese similar to cottage cheese in texture but also quite like halloumi in regards to its firmness. Before adding it to the stir-fry sauce, I like to shallow-fry the cheese cubes on all sides because the caramelized edges add a lovely 'nutty' flavour to the dish. Translated, 'kadhai' means 'wok', which is honestly the best pan to use for this dish. You want the oil to be smoking hot to create a flavoursome curry.

4 tablespoons vegetable oil

500 g/1 lb. 2 oz. paneer, diced

1 teaspoon coriander seeds

1 teaspoon ginger paste

a 2.5-cm/1-inch squared piece of fresh root ginger, cut into julienne

1 large onion, cut into 8 wedges

2 teaspoons salt

½ teaspoon ground turmeric

2 large tomatoes, finely chopped (core and seeds removed)

2 teaspoons tomato purée/paste

1 whole red (bell) pepper, deseeded and cut into wedges

1 whole green (bell) pepper, deseeded and cut into wedges

1 teaspoon dried fenugreek leaves

2 tablespoons freshly chopped coriander/ cilantro (leaves from a small bunch)

2–3 fresh green chillies/ chiles, sliced

KADHAI SPICE

1 teaspoon whole coriander seeds

3 dried chillies/chiles

SERVES 5

For the kadhai spice, toast the coriander seeds and chillies/chiles in a pan over medium heat until the spices become fragrant and aromatic. Blitz the spices in a coffee or spice grinder to make the spice blend, or pound using a pestle and mortar. (You will need 2 teaspoons of the spice blend.)

In a large wok over medium heat, heat the vegetable oil and seal the paneer on all sides. Remove from the pan and drain on paper towels.

Keeping the oil in the pan, fry the coriander seeds until they begin to sizzle. Add the ginger paste and ginger julienne and stir-fry until they start to brown slightly. Add the onion wedges and salt and stir-fry until they are cooked through but not too soft. This is a stir-fry dish, so you want the vegetables to retain a little bite.

Add 2 teaspoons of the kadhai spice blend and the turmeric and mix well for 1 minute. Add the tomatoes and tomato purée/paste and cook through until the tomatoes have melted and softened.

Add the (bell) peppers and 200 ml/¾ cup of water, mix well and cook through over low heat with the lid on for 3–4 minutes. This sauce base is a 'coating sauce', so it shouldn't be too runny. Add the paneer and fenugreek leaves and mix well.

Garnish the kadhai with freshly chopped coriander/ cilantro and green chillies/chiles and serve.

GOSHT ALOO SAAG MASALA

Now this is a dish you will find on most curry house menus; and for me, its certainly a curry house winner! The term 'gosht' refers to 'tender meat' and for this dish, its so important that the meat is cooked until soft and tender, until falling off the bone. More widely known, 'aloo' is potato and 'saag' is spinach. Tender lamb, soft potatoes and a velvety smooth spinach purée all simmered together in an aromatic masala sauce... it tastes as delicious as it sounds!

1 kg/2¼ lbs. leg of lamb on the bone, portioned into pieces

rice or naan bread, to serve (Nitisha's Nutty Naans, page 11)

MARINADE

5 tablespoons vegetable oil

2 teaspoons salt

2 teaspoons Holy Trinity Paste (page 12)

1 teaspoon ground turmeric

1 teaspoon ground cumin

1 teaspoon ground coriander

1 teaspoon Kashmiri red chilli/chili powder

1 teaspoon garam masala

2 tablespoons natural/plain yogurt

1 teaspoon gram/chickpea flour

CURRY SAUCE

6 tablespoons vegetable oil

a 1.5-cm/½-inch piece of cassia bark

2 star anise

6 cloves

6 cardamom pods

1 teaspoon cumin seeds

1 tablespoon fine julienne of fresh root ginger

3 garlic cloves, thinly sliced

2 large onions, finely chopped

1 teaspoon salt

3 tablespoons tomato purée/paste

1 large tomato, chopped (core and seeds removed)

5 potatoes (Maris Piper or Yukon Gold, about 430 g/15 oz. in total), peeled and quartered

1 teaspoon garam masala

1 tablespoon freshly chopped coriander/cilantro

1 tablespoon freshly chopped mint

freshly squeezed juice of ½ lemon

SPINACH PURÉE

400 g/14 oz. fresh baby spinach leaves

1 tablespoon ghee, melted

SERVES 6

Combine all of the ingredients for the marinade in a large mixing bowl, add the lamb and stir to coat. Set aside at room temperature for 30 minutes, then refrigerate for a minimum of 24 hours.

To make the curry sauce, heat the oil in a heavy-bottomed pan over medium heat, add the cassia bark, star anise, cloves and cardamom pods. Fry for 1 minute to release the natural oils, then add the cumin seeds and fry for a further 1 minute.

Add the ginger and garlic and fry until light-brown. Add the onions and salt and fry gently until completely softened and golden-brown. (This may take 25–30 minutes, but be patient and allow the onions to fry slowly.)

Add the marinated lamb, mix well and cook for 30 minutes, stirring occasionally, to seal the meat.

Add the tomato purée/paste, stir in and allow to simmer for 3 minutes. Add the tomato and cook for 15 minutes or until the tomato completely melts into the sauce. Once the sauce has become nice and rich, add 1 litre/quart of water and the potatoes. Cover with a lid, reduce the heat and simmer for 30 minutes until the potatoes are cooked.

To make the spinach purée, put the baby spinach into a food processor and pour in the melted ghee. Blitz the spinach and ghee together until the mixture forms a purée. Set aside.

Add the garam masala, fresh coriander/cilantro, mint, spinach purée and lemon juice to the sauce and mix well. Remove from the heat and serve with rice or naan bread.

MACHHIWAD NI MACHI

Being a Gujarati girl I wanted to showcase a recipe close to my roots. In Gujarat, my family live quite near the coast, the closest fishing village to us is called Machhiwad. And so, here it is, my Machhiwad ni machi which translates to 'fish from Machhiwad'. It is a simple fish curry cooked in a tomato and tamarind sauce with curry leaves, cumin seeds, mustard seeds and fenugreek seeds. For this recipe, I use hake steaks. I think hake is quite an underrated fish and both the flavour and the firmness of the flesh lends itself really well to this curry.

6 x 2.5-cm/1-inch-thick hake steaks (roughly 150 g/5 oz. each)
Roti Breads (page 11), to serve

MARINADE
3 tablespoons vegetable oil
1 teaspoon ground turmeric
½ teaspoon salt
½ teaspoon red chilli/chili powder
freshly squeezed juice of ½ lemon

CURRY SAUCE
4 tablespoons vegetable oil
½ teaspoon fenugreek seeds
1 teaspoon mustard seeds
1 teaspoon cumin seeds
20 fresh curry leaves
6 large tomatoes, chopped (core and seeds removed)
1½ teaspoons salt
1 teaspoon Holy Trinity Paste (page 12)
1 teaspoon curry powder
1 teaspoon ground turmeric
1 teaspoon palm sugar/jaggery
1 teaspoon tamarind paste
1 tablespoon freshly chopped coriander/cilantro

SERVES 6

In a mixing bowl, combine all of the ingredients for the marinade. Rub the marinade into the fish steaks and allow to marinate overnight in the refrigerator or at room temperature for 30 minutes.

Once the fish has marinated, make the curry sauce by heating the oil in a heavy-bottomed pan over medium heat. Add the fenugreek seeds and mustard seeds and fry until they sizzle and pop. Add the cumin seeds and allow them to sizzle, too.

Next, add the curry leaves (be careful as they will splatter in the oil). Add the tomatoes and salt, mix well and allow to melt with the seasoned oil. Cover with a lid to help the tomatoes to melt, stirring occasionally. When the tomatoes have melted down and formed a sauce, add the holy trinity paste, mix well and cook for 3–4 minutes to cook out the raw aroma.

Add the curry powder, turmeric and sugar, mix well and allow to cook into the sauce for a further 3–4 minutes. Add the tamarind paste and 200 ml/¾ cup of water and bring to a gentle simmer.

Add the marinated fish steaks and allow them to poach in the thin curry sauce base over medium heat for 8–10 minutes. Avoid stirring the sauce too much or flipping over the fish steaks at this stage, as you don't want to damage the pieces.

Once the fish steaks are cooked, remove from the heat, sprinkle over the freshly chopped coriander/cilantro and serve with roti breads.

DUCK PEPPER STIR-FRY

Over the last few years I have seen dishes like this pop up on more and more restaurant menus. It would appear that there is a growing trend towards stir-fry dishes and a decline in typical, traditional curry house-style dishes. The roots of this dish are typical of south India, where a large amount of duck is eaten. This recipe has a wonderful stir-fried base flavour from the mustard seeds, curry leaves and ginger, and the duck is cooked for just minutes, which means it is beautifully pink and tender. Taking inspiration from Chinese stir-fry dishes, the sauce is finished off with the addition of a cornflour/cornstarch and water mix.

2 duck breasts, cut into 1-cm/½-inch slices (skin on)

MARINADE
1 teaspoon salt
3 tablespoons vegetable oil
½ teaspoon ground turmeric
½ teaspoon garam masala
1 teaspoon crushed black pepper
¼ teaspoon dried chilli/hot red pepper flakes

SAUCE
3 tablespoons vegetable oil
1 teaspoon mustard seeds
a 2.5-cm/1-inch squared piece of fresh root ginger, thinly sliced
2 garlic cloves, thinly sliced
30 fresh curry leaves
2 dried red chillies/chiles
2 red onions, cut into wedges
½ teaspoon salt
½ teaspoon cracked black pepper
100 g/3½ oz. green/French beans, cut in half
2 teaspoons cornflour/cornstarch

SERVES 4

In a mixing bowl, combine all of the ingredients for the marinade, add the duck slices and mix well. Put in the refrigerator to marinate for 24 hours if possible or for a minimum of 30 minutes if not.

Once the duck has been marinated, prepare the sauce. Heat the oil in a wok or heavy-bottomed pan over medium heat, add the mustard seeds and allow them to crackle and sizzle. Add the ginger and garlic, and fry until golden-brown. Add the curry leaves and red chillies/chiles to the wok and fry for no longer than 7–10 seconds. Add a splash of the water, no more than 100 ml/⅓ cup, just to loosen the wok.

Add the onion wedges, salt and pepper and fry for 6–8 minutes over medium heat until the onion wedges begin to soften slightly. For this dish, you want the onions to retain some bite and not become too soft. Add the green/French beans, mix well and cook for 1 minute (do not overcook the beans as they are best eaten with some bite). Add the marinated duck and mix well to seal the duck all over, then stir in the wok for 5 minutes.

Mix the cornflour/cornstarch and remaining 150 ml/⅔ cup of water together, add to the pan and mix well. Cook for 3–4 minutes, stirring, then serve.

MALABARI MUSSELS

Moules marinière was one of the first dishes I learnt to cook at university as a Culinary Arts Management student. Ever since then I have loved mussels. Here is my Malabari mussels recipe; mussels in a spicy coconut sauce flavoured with curry leaves and mustard seeds. The spice of the chillies/chiles and the aromatic flavour of the curry leaves complement the wonderful saltiness of the mussels ever so well. I like to eat the mussels and then mop up the left over sauce with roti or naan bread.

4 tablespoons vegetable oil
1 teaspoon mustard seeds
30 fresh curry leaves
½ onion, finely chopped
2 green chillies/chiles, thinly sliced
1 teaspoon salt
1 teaspoon ground turmeric
400-ml/14-oz. can coconut milk
500 g/1 lb. 2 oz. mussels (sorted, cleaned and de-bearded)
freshly squeezed juice of ½ lime
1 tablespoon freshly chopped coriander/cilantro
naan bread, to serve (Nitisha's Nutty Naans, page 11)

SERVES 4

Heat the vegetable oil in a heavy-bottomed pan, add the mustard seeds and allow to sizzle and crackle. Add the curry leaves, being careful as they will splatter in the hot oil. Add the onion, chillies/chiles and salt and fry for 10–12 minutes until the onion begins to soften.

Once the onion has softened (it doesn't necessarily have to colour for this recipe), add the turmeric and stir well for 2 minutes to cook out the spice. Add the coconut milk and mix well for 5 minutes.

Add the mussels and 3 tablespoons of water, cover with a lid and cook until the mussels open up. Discard any that do not open. Pour in the lime juice and sprinkle over the freshly chopped coriander/cilantro.

Serve as an appetizer with slices of naan bread to mop up the coconut and mussel liquor.

KADHI PAKORI

Every time I mention this dish to my friends and fellow foodie followers they all have the same expression… 'pakoras in a sauce!?' But I can assure you, this dish is a credit to north (Punjab) and west (Gujarat) India. The crispy pakoras are beautiful when eaten alone as a snack, but when soaked in this tasty, creamy, spiced-yogurt sauce, they take on a completely different nature. Despite being a rather traditional Indian dish, it also has quite a modern appeal to it.

2 tablespoons vegetable oil, plus extra oil for deep-frying
125 g/1⅓ cups gram/chickpea flour
1 large onion, thinly sliced
100 g/3½ oz. boiled, diced potato
2 green chillies/chiles, thinly sliced
1 teaspoon salt
½ teaspoon ground turmeric
½ teaspoon coriander seeds, roasted and crushed
½ teaspoon grated fresh root ginger
¼ teaspoon dried chilli/hot red pepper flakes
¼ teaspoon baking powder
1 tablespoon freshly chopped coriander/cilantro
naan bread, to serve (Nitisha's Nutty Naans, page 11)

SAUCE
1 kg/4¾ cups natural/plain yogurt
2 tablespoons gram/chickpea flour
2 teaspoons salt
2 teaspoons Holy Trinity Paste (page 12)
1 teaspoon ground turmeric
2 tablespoons freshly chopped coriander/cilantro (leaves from a small bunch)
2 tablespoons caster/granulated sugar

SEASONED OIL
3 tablespoons vegetable oil
6 cloves
2 garlic cloves, thinly sliced
2 teaspoons cumin seeds
30 fresh curry leaves
2 green chillies/chiles, thinly sliced
½ teaspoon dried chilli/hot red pepper flakes

deep-fat fryer (optional)

SERVES 6

Start by making the pakoras. Heat the vegetable oil for deep-frying in a deep-fat fryer or large, heavy-bottomed pan to 180°C (350°F). Combine all the ingredients for the pakoras in a mixing bowl and mix well to make a fritter mixture. Using two tablespoons, spoon 1 tablespoon at a time of the fritter mixture into the hot oil in batches of 6–8 to prevent the pan from being over-crowded. Drain the pakoras on paper towels and set aside.

Next, make the sauce by whisking the yogurt, gram/chickpea flour, salt, holy trinity paste and turmeric together in a pan. Whisk to remove the lumps from the flour. Add 500 ml/2 cups of water, the coriander/cilantro and sugar, and whisk again.

Set the pan over low heat and stir continuously to prevent the sauce base from splitting. You need to bring it up to just below boiling point without the sauce splitting or curdling; when it reaches this stage, remove from the heat and set aside.

Make the seasoned oil by heating the oil in a small pan over medium heat. Add the cloves to the hot oil to release the natural aromas, then add the garlic and fry for 30 seconds or until lightly browned. Add the cumin seeds and allow to sizzle. Add the curry leaves, green chillies/chiles and dried chilli/hot red pepper flakes. Pour the oil mixture into the sauce and mix well.

Place the pakoras into the sauce, return the pan to low heat and heat the whole dish up for 2 minutes before serving.

IT'S A CELEBRATION

India is the home of celebration, and whether religious, seasonal or cultural, there is always something to celebrate and groups of people do so at home and in social spaces. With a wide variety of festivals comes a wide variety of celebratory meals. Food is a large part of the Indian culture on a day-to-day basis, but a celebration or a festival is the perfect excuse to take to the kitchen, small or large, and create a feast to please the whole family.

The royal families of India have always been famed for their extravagant meals. With a brigade of classically trained chefs, the royal palace kitchens are renowned for bestowing the royal households with delicious feasts. Just as the British Royals have always enjoyed hunting and feasting on game meats, Indian kings and emperors have followed these traditions. The Achari-spiced Venison on page 68 is marinated in rich spices and yogurt, then sealed in the pan and finished off in the oven to complement the gamey, red meat.

Traditionally, the maharajas and maharanis of India (the princes and their wives) would eat meats that are laced in ghee and slow-roasted, such as the Slow-roasted Leg of Lamb on page 71. They enjoyed dishes that were delicately layered with spices, ranging from basic flavouring ingredients such as ground cumin and coriander, to more luxurious spices such as saffron, which is more expensive by weight than gold! The most popular royal dishes are curries that are finished off with velvety creams and yogurt. The Saffron Murgh Muglai on page 75 is a particularly indulgent curry that can be made in large quantities to feed many people all at once.

This chapter is in itself a celebration of Indian cuisine but with a modern twist. It is a collection of recipes that I cook when celebrating birthdays, anniversaries and festivals. The dishes are at once attractive to look at, to smell in anticipation of an event and to devour together at the table. I hope you will enjoy cooking them as much as I do.

ACHARI-SPICED VENISON

Venison is a wonderfully rich, gamey meat that is also quite lean and reasonably healthy. It has not, however, received the recognition it deserves over the years in the home kitchen. Despite being available in most good butchers and grocery stores, it is not as popular as other meats. The richness of the meat lends itself well to being served as part of a special or formal occasion rather than an average weekday meal. And because of the strength of the meat flavour, the dish needs another boost which will complement the rich gaminess. 'Achar' is the Hindi word for pickle, and it can be used to describe many different types of pickle. For this recipe, I have moved away from traditional chilli/chile-based pickles and created a marinade which still has the main essence of Indian pickle. The marinade tenderizes and flavours the meat and the pungent dry spice rub adds aromatic flavour to the steaks.

2 venison steaks

MARINADE
2 tablespoons vegetable oil
1 tablespoon natural/plain yogurt
½ teaspoon ground turmeric
1 teaspoon gram/chickpea flour
½ teaspoon garam masala
½ teaspoon red chilli/chili powder
½ teaspoon fenugreek powder
½ teaspoon salt
½ teaspoon dried chilli/hot red pepper flakes

DRY RUB
1 teaspoon onion seeds
½ teaspoon ajwain seeds
½ teaspoon rock salt
½ teaspoon crushed black pepper
½ teaspoon cumin seeds

TO SERVE
mashed potatoes (I like to add a pinch of saffron strands for extra flavour)
steamed vegetables of your choosing

SERVES 2

Combine all of the ingredients for the marinade together in a large mixing bowl, mix well and add the venison steaks. Coat the steaks in the marinade and allow them to marinate for 12–24 hours in the refrigerator. If you do not have the time, you can allow the meat to marinate for 30 minutes at room temperature instead.

Preheat the oven to 190°C (375°F) Gas 5.

Mix together all of the ingredients for the dry rub and sprinkle as little or as much as you like over the steaks (bearing in mind that this rub is quite pungent and aromatic). A little sprinkle should be ample.

Set an ovenproof frying pan/skillet over high heat. Seal the steaks in the hot pan on both sides, then transfer to a baking dish. Put the dish in the preheated oven and cook the steaks for 5 minutes or until cooked to your liking.

Allow the steaks to rest for 3 minutes at room temperature, then serve. I like to serve the steaks with some ghee and saffron mashed potatoes and accompanying vegetables.

SLOW-ROASTED LEG OF LAMB

1 leg of lamb
(approximately
1.5–1.7 kg/3½–4 lbs.)

MARINADE

2 teaspoons cumin
seeds

2 teaspoons coriander
seeds

8 tablespoons vegetable
oil

3 teaspoons salt

1 teaspoon crushed
black pepper

1 teaspoon dried chilli/
hot red pepper flakes

1 teaspoon ground
turmeric

1 teaspoon tandoori
powder

1 teaspoon gram/
chickpea flour)

3 large mint sprigs

2 teaspoons Holy Trinity
Paste (page 12)

1 small bunch of
coriander/cilantro
(with stalks)

5 garlic cloves

3 tablespoons natural/
plain yogurt

freshly squeezed juice
of 1 lemon

GRAVY

3 onions, thinly sliced

2 tablespoons plain/
all-purpose flour

baking sheet, lined with
baking parchment

SERVES 6

Over the years, I think this is one dish I have championed. It makes a great 'star of the show' centrepiece for an Indian roast dinner; it's extravagant while also being honest, beautifully cooked and also rustic and 'gnarly'; delicious tasting while also simple to prepare.

In order to achieve a juicy, tender 'fall-off-the-bone' roasted joint, the leg has to be slow-cooked. The leg is left to marinate overnight, allowing the flavours to penetrate through the slashed meat. My tip is to scrape off the marinade before sealing the joint so as not to burn it, then reapply the marinade halfway through cooking. Because the joint is covered with foil while roasting it releases its own liquor, which acts as a lip-smackingly good gravy, and the marinade cooks to form a delicious cross between a cooked rub and glaze!

Start by making the marinade. Toast the cumin and coriander seeds in a dry frying pan/skillet until they become aromatic with an earthy fragrance. Blend all of the marinade ingredients, including the toasted seeds, together in a small food processor or using a pestle and mortar to make a paste. (It can be rather satisfying to pound your own paste for the marinade.)

Using a sharp knife, make deep incisions across the leg of lamb and rub it all over with the marinade paste, paying extra attention to massaging the marinade into the deep cuts for the flavour to penetrate through. Allow the joint to marinate for 24 hours in the refrigerator on the lined baking sheet. (Sometimes the acid in the marinade can react with certain metals, which may cause your meat to pick up an unpleasant flavour, so it is best to protect your meat by lining the baking sheet.)

Preheat the oven to 180°C (350°F) Gas 4.

Scrape off as much of the marinade as you can and reserve to be used later. Seal and brown the joint all over in a pan. Set aside.

For the gravy, put the onions in a roasting pan, add 250 ml/1 cup of water and sprinkle over the flour. Place the sealed lamb joint on top and roast in the preheated oven for 30 minutes.

Cover the roasting pan tightly with foil, then reduce the oven temperature to 150°C (300°F) Gas 2 and allow the joint to slow-roast for 3½ hours.

Remove the joint from the oven and leave to rest, covered, for 15 minutes before serving. The joint must be tender, so that the meat effortlessly falls off the bone when carved.

MASALA LOBSTER

Need a recipe to impress? Well, here you have it. Because lobster is quite an expensive ingredient, I tend to make this dish mostly at Christmas or for very formal and celebratory dinner parties. Many people are afraid to prepare lobster, but it is actually quite easy. The common way to handle lobster would be to boil it and then prepare it, which is absolutely fine. But I feel that by cooking the lobster meat before applying the spice to it, you do not allow the lobster meat to take on the maximum flavour from the spice mix, which is why I prepare the lobsters while still raw. I take great pride when serving this dish.

1 live lobster

MARINADE
2 tablespoons vegetable oil
1 teaspoon Holy Trinity Paste (page 12)
freshly squeezed juice of ½ lemon
1 tablespoon finely chopped coriander/ cilantro
1 teaspoon salt
1 teaspoon ground turmeric
1 teaspoon ground cumin
1 teaspoon ground coriander
1 teaspoon dried chilli/ hot red pepper flakes

TO SERVE
freshly chopped coriander/cilantro
diced red onion
lemon wedges

SERVES 2

The first step is to prepare your lobster. Using frozen lobster is fine, but you won't get the same flavour you would get from using fresh lobster. The first thing to do is to cut the lobster in half directly through the middle. If the lobster is alive, you need to do this quickly and swiftly to inflict as little pain on the lobster as possible. The best way to do this is to use a very sharp knife and stab the lobster through the head. Lobsters naturally have a vertical line running from their head to tail, so use this as a guide and cut along this line. Remove the claws and legs from the lobster (if you are using frozen lobster, make sure it is fully thawed), hold the body tightly with one hand and pull the claws and legs away with your other hand. (The claws aren't required, but if you can, crack and peel away the shell to use just the meat.)

You should be left with two lobster pieces from the head to tail. Now you need to get rid of the gills (also known as 'dead man's fingers') and the stomach sac. The stomach sac and gills are both located directly behind the mouth. The gills look like cream-coloured, long, feathery growths, which aren't poisonous, but are very unpleasant to eat.

Mix all the marinade ingredients together in a bowl. Using a spoon, put as much or as little marinade as you would like onto the lobster halves. The marinade has a medium level of heat, so if you prefer it hotter, increase the amount of holy trinity paste. Once the lobster is marinated, place on a baking sheet, cover with clingfilm/plastic wrap and put in the refrigerator for a minimum of 2 hours and a maximum of 1 day.

Preheat the oven to 180°C (350°F) Gas 4.

Remove the clingfilm/plastic wrap and place the baking sheet in the preheated oven for 15–20 minutes. Check every 5 minutes to make sure that the lobster isn't becoming over-cooked.

Place the cooked lobster halves on a serving dish, sprinkle over the freshly chopped coriander/cilantro and serve with diced onion and lemon wedges.

SAFFRON MURGH MUGLAI

This recipe is based upon the cuisine from the Mughal Empire also known as 'Medieval India'. India has always been famous for its maharajas or kings, and almost every state had its own maharaja and royal family that were treated with utmost respect and love from the kingdom. They only ever ate the best food, prepared by the best chefs in the land. Mughlai cuisine is famous for being elaborate, rich, flavoursome, extravagant and generally not overly spicy. The dish uses ingredients that only the royal family would once be able to enjoy, such as saffron, ghee and a blend of spices that were once used as a currency!

1 kg/2¼ lbs. chicken, diced
3 tablespoons ghee
a 5-cm/2-inch cinnamon or cassia bark stick
5 cloves
3 cardamom pods
1 teaspoon cumin seeds
3 onions, finely chopped
2 teaspoons salt
1 teaspoon Holy Trinity Paste (page 12)
1 teaspoon ground cumin
1 teaspoon ground coriander
1 teaspoon ground turmeric
1 teaspoon paprika
2 tablespoons tomato purée/paste
2 large tomatoes, finely chopped (core and seeds removed)
a good pinch of saffron strands
150 ml/⅔ cup double/heavy cream
100 ml/⅓ cup natural/plain yogurt
1 teaspoon dried fenugreek leaves
1 teaspoon garam masala

MARINADE
3 tablespoons vegetable oil
1 teaspoon Holy Trinity Paste (page 12)
1 teaspoon salt
1 teaspoon ground cumin
1 teaspoon ground coriander
1 teaspoon paprika
1 teaspoon ground turmeric
2 tablespoons natural/plain yogurt
1 teaspoon tomato purée/paste
1 teaspoon garam masala

TO SERVE
freshly chopped coriander/cilantro
boiled rice

SERVES 6

Combine all of the ingredients for the marinade in a large mixing bowl, add the chicken and coat it well. Allow the chicken to marinate for 24 hours in the refrigerator. If you do not have time, you can marinate it for 30 minutes at room temperature.

Heat the ghee in a heavy-bottomed pan over medium heat and allow it to melt. Add the cinnamon stick, cloves and cardamom pods and fry for 1 minute. Add the cumin seeds and heat until they sizzle and pop.

Add the onions and salt and gently fry until soft and buttery; this will take a good 30 minutes, but be patient and allow the onions to really soften. Add a little more ghee or a splash of water if dry.

Add the holy trinity paste, mix and fry for 2–3 minutes. Add the ground spices and a splash more water and fry for 4–5 minutes.

Add the tomato purée/paste, mix well and fry for 2–3 minutes. Add the tomatoes, mix well, cover and cook over low heat for 20 minutes.

Add the marinated chicken and mix really well so that the chicken is well coated with the sauce. Once the chicken is sealed, add 450 ml/scant 2 cups of water and simmer gently for 25–30 minutes.

Next, add the saffron strands, cream and yogurt, mix really well and simmer for a further 5 minutes. Add the fenugreek leaves and garam masala, then stir. Sprinkle with fresh coriander/cilantro and serve with rice.

HARIYALI SALMON

As a lover of seafood, I particularly adore salmon, and believe it has the perfect characteristics to make a splendid, celebratory, centrepiece, especially when smothered in a mouth watering masala! Hariyali is the hindi term for greenery, deriving from the word *hari* (green), here the Hariyali is referring to the super green 'Hariyali masala' which is smothered onto the meaty flesh just before roasting. Although the masala marinade doesn't have as many spices as other typical Indian marinades would, the simple yet robust flavours of the coriander, mint, green chillies, lime juice, garlic and ginger is a perfect balance to compliment the natural richness and 'butteriness' of the salmon.

4 salmon fillets

MARINADE
freshly squeezed juice
  of 1 lime
2 tablespoons vegetable
  oil
1½ teaspoons salt

HARIYALI MASALA
a medium bunch of
  coriander/cilantro
  (about 20 g/¾ oz.)
a medium bunch of
  mint (about 15 g/
  ½ oz.)
20 g/⅓ cup baby
  spinach leaves
1 teaspoon salt
½ teaspoon ground
  coriander
freshly squeezed juice
  of ½ lime

1 tablespoon gram/
  chickpea flour
2 garlic cloves
3 green chillies/chiles
a 2.5-cm/1-inch squared
  piece of fresh root
  ginger
3 tablespoons vegetable
  oil

TO SERVE
freshly chopped
  coriander/cilantro
thinly sliced green
  chilli/chile
boiled rice
lime wedges

SERVES 4

Mix the marinade ingredients together in a large bowl, add the salmon and coat in the marinade. Put in the refrigerator to marinate for 2 hours.

Blend together all of the ingredients for the hariyali masala in a food processor. The masala should be a smooth paste.

Preheat the oven to 180°C (350°F) Gas 4.

Seal the salmon fillets in a hot frying pan/skillet, skin-side down to create a crispy skin. (You still want the salmon to be raw on top, so once the skin is nicely browned, take the fillets out of the pan and set aside on a baking sheet.)

Using a palette knife or a dessertspoon, smear the hariyali masala all over the salmon fillets to coat them evenly. Bake the salmon in the preheated oven for 8–10 minutes. The salmon should be tender and moist.

Serve hot, sprinkled with freshly chopped coriander/cilantro and sliced green chillies/chiles, with boiled rice and lime wedges on the side.

MALAI KOFTAS

Who said vegetarian food can't be celebratory?! This recipe is the perfect example of how to make meat-free dishes luxurious. The koftas are made of chopped-up vegetables and paneer cheese which are lightly spiced and held together with gram/chickpea flour. They are then deep-fried until golden-brown and served in a rich creamy sauce which is also mildly spiced. 'Malai' is the Indian word for 'reduced milk', which is often used for rich and regal dishes such as this. (Also pictured pages 80–81)

KOFTAS

- 100 g/²⁄₃ cup peas, chopped
- ½ carrot, chopped
- 1 onion, chopped
- 80 g/3 oz. paneer, grated
- 250 g/scant 1¼ cups mashed potatoes (Maris Piper or Yukon Gold)
- 1 tablespoon chopped pistachio nuts
- 1 tablespoon chopped peanuts
- 1½ tablespoons gram/chickpea flour
- 1 teaspoon salt
- ½ teaspoon Holy Trinity Paste (page 12)
- ½ teaspoon ground turmeric
- ½ teaspoon ground cumin
- 1 tablespoon unsweetened dessicated/dried shredded coconut
- vegetable oil, for deep-frying
- fresh naan bread or boiled basmati rice, to serve (optional)

MALAI SAUCE

- 4 tablespoons vegetable oil
- 1 onion, finely chopped
- 1 teaspoon salt
- ½ teaspoon Holy Trinity Paste (page 12)
- ½ teaspoon ground turmeric
- 1 teaspoon paprika
- 1 teaspoon ground coriander
- 1 teaspoon ground cumin
- 3 tablespoons tomato purée/paste
- 2 large tomatoes, chopped (core and seeds removed)
- 1 tablespoon natural/plain yogurt
- 250 ml/1 cup double/heavy cream
- 1 tablespoon palm sugar/jaggery
- 1 teaspoon dried fenugreek leaves
- 1 teaspoon garam masala

deep-fat fryer (optional)

SERVES 4

Heat the oil for deep-frying in a deep-fat fryer or large, heavy-bottomed pan to 180°C (350°F).

Combine all of the ingredients for the koftas together in a mixing bowl. Shape the mixture into 16 smooth balls. Deep-fry the balls for 5–6 minutes or until golden-brown and cooked through. Transfer to paper towels to drain any excess oil.

For the malai sauce, heat the oil in a heavy-bottomed pan over low heat, add the onion and salt and gently fry until softened. Do not allow it to colour too much as you want the onion to retain its sweetness. (Cooking the onion should take 20–25 minutes.)

Add the holy trinity paste and fry until the strong raw aroma has been cooked away. Add the ground spices and mix well into the onions. Cook out the spices until they are no longer pungent, adding a splash of water if necessary.

Add the tomato purée/paste, mix well and gently fry for 3 minutes.

Add the tomatoes and cook until they have melted down; about 15–20 minutes.

Whisk the yogurt so that it is creamy with no lumps and pour into the pan with the cream and 150 ml/²⁄₃ cup of water. Simmer gently for 5–6 minutes, mixing well to make a sauce.

Add the palm sugar/jaggery, fenugreek leaves and garam masala and mix in well. Finally, add the koftas and allow to heat through in the sauce.

Serve with fresh naan bread or basmati rice.

SWEET AND SOUR MALLARD BREAST

Inspired by one of my most favourite Chinese dishes, sweet and sour duck, here is my take on the much loved classic. Being a rich gamey meat, duck makes a great dish to serve at special occasions. As beautiful as duck breast is on its own, it's no secret that when paired with strong, punchy flavours, duck is elevated even further. And this dish certainly delivers on strong, punchy flavours. Where the dry rub packs in seasoning, heat and a wonderful floral aroma, the glaze imparts a sticky, savoury, umami coating.

2 duck breasts

DRY RUB
½ teaspoon rock salt
½ teaspoon crushed black pepper
½ teaspoon dried chilli/ hot red pepper flakes
¼ teaspoon ground star anise

GLAZE
3 tablespoons vegetable oil
2 garlic cloves, finely diced
a 1.5-cm/½-inch piece of fresh root ginger, finely diced
3 tablespoons soy sauce
½ teaspoon dried chilli/ hot red pepper flakes
2 tablespoons palm sugar/jaggery
6 tablespoons tamarind paste

TO SERVE
Masala Roasted Potatoes (page 99)
steamed green/French beans

SERVES 2

Mix all the dry rub ingredients together. Coat the duck breasts with it and allow to marinate at room temperature for 15–30 minutes. (This recipe does not require a long marinating time.)

Preheat the oven to 190°C (375°F) Gas 5. Put a baking sheet in the oven to heat up.

Next, make the glaze. Heat the oil in a pan over low heat, add the garlic and ginger and fry until lightly browned and no longer raw. Add the soy sauce, 50 ml/3½ tablespoons of water and the dried chilli/hot red pepper flakes. Gently simmer for 4–5 minutes.

Stir in the palm sugar/jaggery and tamarind paste and allow to simmer gently for 4–5 minutes over low heat. Remove from the heat and set aside.

Lay the duck breasts skin-side down in a separate cold pan (this will render the fat out more efficiently than a hot pan, which will lock in all of the fatty juices). Gradually turn the heat up and cook the breasts for 3 minutes. Flip over and seal the raw side to lock in all the juices. (90 per cent of the pan-cooking must be done skin-side down.)

Transfer the duck breasts to the preheated baking sheet and roast in the preheated oven for 6 minutes. Remove the baking sheet from the oven and allow the breasts to rest on the hot sheet for 4 minutes. Slice the breasts, drizzle the glaze over the top and serve with masala roasted potatoes and green/French beans.

SAGAR'S MASALA FISH PIE

This is a recipe which I hold very close to my heart as it is named after my little brother Sagar. 'Sagar' in Hindi means 'the ocean' and coincidentally, my little brother is a big fan of seafood. Seafood is a favourite in my family, but born and bred in Britain we also have a collection of classic British dishes as our favourites, too. This recipe is the perfect example of Indian and British fusion food. The spiced, marinated seafood is cooked in a rich, creamy south-Indian-inspired coconut sauce, and topped off with a mustard-seed seasoned mashed potato. This masala fish pie certainly delivers on both flavour and theatre when served at the table. (Pictured page 87)

MARINATED FISH MIX
500 g/1 lb. 2 oz.
    (approximately 16)
    fresh raw king
    prawns/jumbo
    shrimp (heads and
    shells removed)
200 g/7 oz. scallops
300 g/10½ oz. salmon,
    cut into 2.5-cm/1-inch
    cubes
200 g/7 oz. cod, cut into
    2.5-cm/1-inch cubes
4 tablespoons vegetable
    oil
grated zest from
    ½ lemon
1 teaspoon salt
a pinch of saffron
    strands
½ teaspoon Holy Trinity
    Paste (page 12)
½ teaspoon ground
    turmeric

SOUTH-INDIAN
CURRY SAUCE
5 tablespoons vegetable
    oil
1 teaspoon mustard
    seeds
1 teaspoon cumin seeds
1 teaspoon finely diced
    fresh root ginger
2 garlic cloves, finely
    diced
20 fresh curry leaves
2 large onions, finely
    chopped
2 teaspoons salt
2 teaspoons ground
    cumin
2 teaspoons ground
    coriander
2 teaspoons ground
    turmeric
2 teaspoons paprika
¼ teaspoon dried chilli/
    hot red pepper flakes
1 tablespoon tomato
    purée/paste
3 tomatoes, chopped
    (core and seeds
    removed)

1 teaspoon palm sugar/
    jaggery
400-ml/14-oz. can
    coconut milk
2 teaspoons cornflour/
    cornstarch
1 teaspoon garam
    masala
1 tablespoon freshly
    chopped coriander/
    cilantro

TOPPING
1.2 kg/2¾ lbs. floury
    white potatoes (Maris
    Piper or Yukon Gold)
1 kg/2¼ lbs. sweet
    potatoes

MASH SEASONING
5 tablespoons ghee
1 teaspoon mustard
    seeds
10 fresh curry leaves

*a disposable piping/pastry
bag
32 x 14 x 6 cm/13 x 5½ x
2½-inch ovenproof dish*

SERVES 6–8

Combine all of the ingredients for the marinated fish mix in a large mixing bowl. Cover and put in the refrigerator to marinate overnight. If you do not have the time, allow the seafood to marinate for 30 minutes at room temperature instead.

To make the sauce, heat the oil in a heavy-bottomed pan over medium heat, add the mustard seeds and cook until they crackle and sizzle. Add the cumin seeds and fry until they pop.

Add the ginger and garlic and fry gently for 20 seconds just to remove the raw aroma; they don't have to be browned. Add the curry leaves, quickly stir and add in the onions and salt. Fry the onions gently until they become soft, covering with a lid to help the process.

Add the ground cumin, coriander, turmeric paprika and dried chilli/hot red pepper flakes and cook until they have lost their raw aroma. Add a splash of water if the pan starts to dry out.

Add the tomato purée/paste, mix well and simmer for 3–4 minutes. Add the tomatoes and cook, covered, until they have completely melted down to form a sauce, stirring occasionally.

Add the palm sugar/jaggery and coconut milk and simmer for 5 minutes. Mix the cornflour/cornstarch with a little water and stir into the sauce to thicken. Allow the sauce to simmer for 3–4 minutes.

Add the garam masala and freshly chopped coriander/cilantro, mix well and allow the sauce to cool completely.

Meanwhile, prepare the topping by boiling the potatoes in separate pans – the floury white potatoes will need 20–25 minutes to soften, while the sweet potatoes will need 15–20 minutes. When soft enough to mash, drain both potatoes and mash together in a large mixing bowl. Transfer the mixture to a disposable piping/pastry bag and snip off the end.

Preheat the oven to 180°C (350°F) Gas 4.

Once the sauce has cooled, it is time to assemble the pie. Lay out the marinated fish in the bottom of the ovenproof dish so that it is evenly distributed (every serving should have a selection of different pieces of seafood). Pour over the cooled sauce. Pipe on the mashed potato topping (you can do this with a spoon or spatula if you prefer, although this may be slightly messy as it can mix in with the sauce).

Prepare the mash seasoning. Heat up the ghee in a pan, add the mustard seeds and fry until they sizzle and pop. Add the curry leaves, then remove the pan from the heat. Spoon the seasoning evenly over the pie.

Bake the masala fish pie in the preheated oven for 25–30 minutes or until the fish is cooked through. Serve hot.

TANDOORI SPATCHCOCK POUSSIN

Tandoori cookery is an Indian style of cooking that involves grilling marinated meat over an intense fire in a *tandoor*, a traditional clay oven. The flavour imparted from Tandoori cooking is smoky, earthy, gnarly and for a better word 'charcoaly'. I wanted to create a dish, which whilst paying homage to the traditional cooking method and flavours, also presents a more modern and lighter offering. Rather than using a whole chicken, I have used spatchcocked poussin, a beautiful bird which takes a quarter of the time to cook.

2 whole poussins
8 tablespoons vegetable oil
1 tablespoon Holy Trinity Paste (page 12)
2 tablespoons natural/plain yogurt
2 teaspoons ground cumin
2 teaspoons ground coriander
1 teaspoon ground turmeric
2 teaspoons paprika
1½ teaspoons salt
1 teaspoon cumin seeds
freshly squeezed juice of ½ lemon
2 tablespoons freshly chopped coriander/cilantro (leaves from a small bunch)
1 teaspoon dried chilli/hot red pepper flakes
2 teaspoons dried fenugreek leaves
1 teaspoon toasted gram/chickpea flour)

TO SERVE
Tomato, Cucumber and Mint Raita (page 130)
Mango and Chilli/Chile Salsa (page 130)
¼ red onion, thinly sliced
¼ cucumber, sliced
freshly chopped coriander/cilantro

SERVES 2

Lay the poussins breast-side down on a chopping board. Using a pair of sharp scissors, cut along the side of the spine bone on both sides and remove it. (You can ask your butcher to do this for you if you wish.)

Gently pull the poussin by the legs and flatten it so that the skin-side of the bird is facing you. Place both poussins flat on a baking sheet, skin-side up.

Combine all of the remaining ingredients to make your marinade. Marinate the poussins by rubbing the marinade all over, getting into all the nooks and crannies. Put in the refrigerator to marinate for a minimum of 1 hour or, if possible, overnight.

Preheat the oven to 180°C (350°F) Gas 4.

Heat a griddle pan and char each poussin on both sides. Place the poussins back onto the baking sheet and roast in the preheated oven for 30 minutes, until cooked, turning over halfway through.

Serve with tomato, cucumber and mint raita, mango and chilli salsa and a mixed salad of red onion, cucumber and fresh coriander/cilantro.

GOSHT DUM BIRIYANI

This is a very traditional dish in India, it has Persian roots and is the perfect example of a celebratory dish. What makes this biriyani stand out so much is the fact that it is prepared in stages and it is layered, then covered with a pastry lid which locks in all of the steam and flavour. The concept is extremely clever and the dish has been cooked in this way for centuries. The flavour is enhanced with rich fried onions which have a wonderful caramelized flavour, and also with a saffron-infused milk which adds an earthy aroma that is carried through the whole dish. (Pictured pages 92 and 93)

1 kg/2¼ lbs. lamb leg on the bone, diced
600 g/3½ cups basmati rice (rinsed and soaked in 1.2 litres/ quarts cold water for 30 minutes)
2 tablespoons ghee
6 cardamom pods
2 bay leaves
a 5-cm/2-inch cinnamon stick
8 cloves
1 teaspoon cumin seeds
Crispy Fried Onions (page 12)
Mango and Chilli/Chile Salsa (page 130), to serve

MARINADE
1 tablespoon Holy Trinity Paste (page 12)
4 tablespoons natural/ plain yogurt
5 tablespoons oil from the Crispy Fried Onions (page 12)
1 teaspoon Kashmiri red chilli/chili powder
1 teaspoon ground turmeric
1 teaspoon ground cumin
1 teaspoon ground coriander
1 teaspoon paprika
freshly squeezed juice of ½ lemon
1 tablespoon freshly chopped coriander/ cilantro
1 tablespoon freshly chopped mint
3 teaspoons salt
2 teaspoons garam masala

SAFFRON-INFUSED MILK
a pinch of saffron strands
4 tablespoons full-fat/ whole milk

PASTRY
300 g/2⅓ cups plain/ all-purpose flour
1 egg, beaten, to glaze
cumin seeds, to sprinkle

14 x 7.5-cm/5½ x 3-inch ovenproof dish or stainless steel pan

SERVES 8

Combine all of the marinade ingredients in a large mixing bowl. Add the lamb and allow to marinate for 24 hours in the refrigerator. If you do not have the time, you can allow the meat to marinate for 30 minutes at room temperature instead.

The next step is to cook the rice so that it is half-cooked. Drain away the water from the soaked rice and rinse to remove any excess starch; this may take 5–6 washes. Bring 2 litres/quarts of water to the boil in a saucepan, add the rice and cook over medium heat for 6–7 minutes or until you can tell that the grains are half-cooked. Drain the rice, rinse under cold water gently (not for too long, just enough to bring the temperature down to warm rather than hot) and set aside until required.

In another pan, you need to cook the lamb. As it is lamb on the bone, we need to ensure the meat is tender, and the best way to do this is to cook it prior to putting it in the biriyani. Start by heating the ghee in a heavy-bottomed pan over medium heat, adding the cardamom pods, bay leaves, cinnamon and cloves, and frying to release the natural aromatic flavours and oils. Add the cumin seeds and allow to sizzle and crackle. Add the lamb and mix really well on a high heat to seal the pieces all over. This will lock in all of the flavour and juices. (Do not discard any debris left in the marinating bowl. Deglaze the bowl with some water and add this to the pan as well.)

Once the lamb is sealed, it should start to release natural juices, so at this stage, add 500 ml/ 2 cups of water, reduce the heat to medium and cover with a lid. Allow the lamb to simmer for 45 minutes, stirring occasionally. The natural cooking liquor is great to use in the biriyani so don't allow this to burn off.

To make the saffron-infused milk, add the saffron strands to the milk and set aside for 2–3 minutes.

The pastry is not eaten, so the flavour and texture do not matter. I like to sprinkle cumin seeds over mine so that it looks more visually appealing when presenting at the dinner table. Mix the flour with 150 ml/⅔ cup of water and bring together into a dough. Set aside, covered.

Preheat the oven to 150°C (300°F) Gas 2.

Because this is a layered biriyani, it is important to have all of the components ready before you start. In the bottom of your ovenproof dish, place some of the lamb (with the excess cooking juices). Scatter over some of the half-cooked rice, sprinkle over some of the crispy fried onions, and drizzle over some of the cooking liquor and about 1 tablespoon of the saffron-infused milk. Repeat this process at least twice or until your dish is full and you have used up all of the ingredients.

Roll out the pastry into a circle that is larger than the top of your dish. Place the pastry lid on top of the dish and gently crimp the edges, squeezing tightly to cover any gaps from where steam may escape. Brush with beaten egg and sprinkle with cumin seeds.

Put the dish in the middle of the preheated oven and bake for 45 minutes until cooked through. (The benefit of pre-cooking the components is that it means each element will cook at the same time once in the oven.)

Allow the biriyani to sit for 2 minutes once you have removed it from the oven. Remove the pastry lid and discard. Using a large spoon, gently fold the biriyani but do not over-mix.

Serve immediately with mango and chilli salsa.

VEGETARIAN DISHES AND SIDES

Ever since I was a little girl, I have been fascinated by the concept of the tiffin. The way the compartments stack on top of one another reminds me of a magical, old, shiny jewellery box that is full of tasty treats.

Mahadeo Havaji Bachche, an Indian entrepreneur, started the tiffin distribution business in 1890 to meet the demands of Mumbai's growing working population. Supposedly, by the 1950s the tiffin-wallahs who delivered food to workers were delivering some 200,000 tiffins a day. In the late 18th century, when India was under British rule, a lot of lifestyle changes were slowly beginning to take place. One of the main influences of the British raj was the way in which Indians ate and encouraged them to have lighter meals at lunchtimes.

With food being such an enormous part of India's culture and lifestyle, home-cooked food is highly regarded and renowned for being cooked with a great deal of love and care. Eating food that has been cooked at home is always seen to be the best option because people prefer to know what they are eating – it is generally healthier and also much cheaper which is always a bonus!

On most occasions, lunch is served as a selection of tasty regional treats known as a 'thali', which is much like Indian tapas.

With Indian food being as diverse as it is with lots of different vegetables, curries, pulses and breads, a one-compartment lunchbox simply would not work.

Tiffins or 'dhabbas' come in all shapes and sizes. Usually, they are round in shape with three or four compartments that stack on top of one another. The tiffin is firmly sealed on top with a firm-fitting lid, a clip to avoid any spillages and a handle on top for convenience.

Eating from a tiffin is hugely popular all over India. From office workers in busy cities to women working from dusk till dawn in crop fields and children taking a packed lunch with them to enjoy at school, the tiffin serves a purpose for all of them.

The contents of a tiffin varies depending on the region; in south India and Nepal, the Tiffin is generally a between-meal snack box consisting of wrapped-up dosas and idlis, which are savoury cakes. In other parts of India such as Mumbai, the term 'tiffin', mostly refers to a packed lunch of some sort that usually consists of rice, dhal, curry, vegetables, chapatis and sometimes spicy meats too. However you choose to pack your tiffin, you'll be sure to find inspiration with the recipes for vegetarian and side dishes in this chapter.

KAALI DHAL

300 g/1½ cups urad
   dhal, soaked in
   2 litres/quarts water
   overnight
100 g/generous ½ cup
   dried red kidney
   beans, soaked in
   2 litres/quarts water
   overnight
5 tablespoons vegetable
   oil
1 tablespoon ginger
   paste
1 tablespoon garlic paste
1 onion, finely chopped
1 teaspoon salt
1 teaspoon Holy Trinity
   Paste (page 12)
½ teaspoon each of
   ground coriander,
   ground cumin and
   ground turmeric
1 teaspoon tomato
   purée/paste
3 large tomatoes,
   chopped (core and
   seeds removed)
50 g/3½ tablespoons
   butter
2 tablespoons double/
   heavy cream
1 teaspoon dried
   fenugreek leaves
1 tablespoon freshly
   chopped coriander/
   cilantro
1 teaspoon garam
   masala
Seasoned Oil (page 12)
roti breads, to serve

SERVES 6

I'm an avid fan of lentils, not only are they high in protein, but they're also very tasty and have a great texture, too. 'Kaali dhal', literally translates to 'black dhal' because of the dark colour of the urad dhal used in this recipe. Here, I use three parts of urad dhal to one part of kidney beans. (It is important to soak the lentils and beans overnight because it improves and softens the texture – canned pulses are not suitable for dhals.) Moreish, savoury and accented with a rich sauce that brings harmony to this dhal.

Drain the soaked lentils and rinse them well, then transfer to a pressure cooker with 1.5 litres/quarts of the water. Drain the red kidney beans and add these as well. Cook until the lentils are falling apart, this should take about 3–4 whistles (or 15 minutes) depending on your pressure cooker guidelines. (Alternatively, you can boil them in a pan, but this can take up to 4 hours.)

Heat the vegetable oil in a pan over low–medium heat and fry out the ginger and garlic pastes until the raw aroma has been cooked off and the shreds begin to separate from one another. Add the onion and salt and fry really well so that the onions are buttery soft and golden-brown; this will take a good 30 minutes.

Now that we have created a caramelized base flavour to the sauce, we add the holy trinity paste to add a fresh heat in the dish. Fry the paste in the onion mix for 3–4 minutes to cook through. Add the ground spices and cook for 3–4 minutes; add a splash of water if the pan starts to dry out slightly. Add the tomato purée/paste, mix well and fry for 2 minutes, then add the tomatoes and mix really well. Cover with a lid and gently simmer to allow the tomatoes to melt down to form a rich sauce.

Add the cooked lentils and mix really well. Loosen the sauce with more of water to your desired consistency, I like my dhals quite thin, so I would add about 1 litre/quart water at this stage.

We need to add another depth to the dhal by adding all of the finishing ingredients which will increase the richness. Add the butter, double/heavy cream, dried fenugreek leaves, freshly chopped coriander/cilantro and garam masala. Mix really well and let the dhal slowly simmer on an extremely low heat for 10–15 minutes.

If you haven't yet prepared the seasoned oil, now is the time to do so. Pour the seasoned oil on top of the dhal, scraping every last bit out.

Mix well, and serve immediately with fresh roti breads.

MASALA ROASTED POTATOES

Ever since my school dinner days, I have loved a good roasted potato and, having worked in various food places from canteens to restaurants, I have always appreciated the simplicity that goes into creating a good 'roastie'. But, if anything, I love the satisfaction from the end result more. This recipe is a true representation of British and Indian fusion food, the cooking process is completely British, but the flavours and ingredients scream India. These are best served with a fish curry or lamb curry and even work well as a replacement for chips/fries.

1 kg/2¼ lbs. potatoes (Maris Piper or Yukon Gold), peeled and cut into quarters or equal pieces

SPICE MIX
5 tablespoons vegetable oil
1 teaspoon cumin seeds
1 teaspoon mustard seeds
1 teaspoon coriander seeds
5 garlic cloves, unpeeled
½ teaspoon dried chilli/hot red pepper flakes
1 teaspoon coarse sea salt

SERVES 6

Preheat the oven to 180°C (350°F) Gas 4.

Cook the potatoes in a pan of salted boiling water for 20 minutes or until soft. Drain away the excess water and leave in a colander to steam. Shake the colander around to allow the potatoes to fluff up and become slightly rough and rustic around the edges (this will make the potatoes more crispy).

Add all of the ingredients for the spice mix into a roasting pan and place in the preheated oven for 5 minutes to allow all of the spices to infuse into the oil.

Remove the pan from the oven and add the potatoes, being careful not to splash any hot oil. Coat the potatoes well in the oil, then put the pan back into the oven and roast for 20–30 minutes until golden-brown all over. Toss the potatoes occasionally to ensure even cooking.

Serve as an accompaniment.

GUJARATI TADKA TUVAAR/TOOR DHAL

Toor dhal is another celebration of the humble lentil. Lentils are a staple in Indian cuisine as they are so accessible, cheap and versatile. For me, this dish is the ultimate comfort food and it goes well with rice or on its own as a soup. To boost the healthiness of the dish, I like to include vegetables such as carrots, tomatoes and aubergines/eggplants. I like to take the dimension of the dhal to another level by introducing flavours such as palm sugar/jaggery for sweetness and fresh lime for a citrusy finish.

TUVAAR/TOOR DHAL

100 g/½ cup tuvaar/ toor lentils, soaked overnight
½ carrot, grated
2 tomatoes, cut into quarters
1 small aubergine/ eggplant, peeled and cut into 1-cm/³∕₈-inch chunks
10 peanuts
1 tablespoon grated fresh root ginger
1 teaspoon Holy Trinity Paste (page 12)
¼ teaspoon fenugreek seeds
2 teaspoons salt
½ teaspoon ground turmeric
½ teaspoon ground cumin
1 teaspoon ground coriander

SEASONED OIL

5 tablespoons vegetable oil
½ cassia bark or cinnamon stick
5 cloves
1 teaspoon mustard seeds
¼ teaspoon fenugreek seeds
1 teaspoon cumin seeds
6 cashew nut halves
2 green chillies/chiles, slit
½ teaspoon asafoetida
10 fresh curry leaves

TO SERVE

1 tablespoon palm sugar/jaggery
1 tablespoon freshly chopped coriander/ cilantro
freshly squeezed juice of ½ lemon
naan bread or cooked rice

SERVES 6

For the dhal, drain the soaked lentils and rinse them well, then transfer them to a pressure cooker with all the other ingredients for the dhal and 750 ml/3 cups of water. Place the lid on and cook under pressure for 3 whistles; around 15 minutes depending on your pressure cooker guidelines. (If you do not have a pressure cooker, you can boil them in a pan, but this can take up to 4 hours for the same result.)

Once the dhal base is cooked, blitz everything together using a stick blender. The base will thicken considerably, so add some water to achieve your desired consistency. Set aside while you prepare the seasoned oil.

Heat the oil in a small, heavy-bottomed pan over medium heat, add the cassia bark and cloves and fry to release the natural aromatic oils and fragrances. Add the mustard and fenugreek seeds and fry until they begin to sizzle. Add the cumin seeds and allow them to sizzle and pop, too. Add the cashew nut halves and allow to brown slightly in the hot oil. Add the green chillies/chiles and toss in the oil. Stir in the asafoetida and curry leaves, give everything a really good mix and pour over the dhal base.

Mix the dhal well to bring all of the ingredients together. Finish by adding in the palm sugar/ jaggery, coriander/cilantro and lime juice. Serve immediately with either fresh naan bread or rice.

CHANNA MASALA

6 tablespoons vegetable
  oil
3 cloves
1 teaspoon each of
  mustard seeds and
  cumin seeds
½ teaspoon fenugreek
  seeds
2 teaspoons each of
  finely diced fresh root
  ginger and garlic
8–10 fresh curry leaves
2 onions, finely diced
1 teaspoon salt
1 teaspoon Holy Trinity
  Paste (page 12)
1 teaspoon each of
  ground turmeric,
  ground cumin,
  ground coriander
  and paprika
1 tablespoon tomato
  purée/paste
5 tomatoes, chopped
6 tablespoons Boiled
  Onion Purée (page 12)
2 cans black chickpeas,
  drained
2 teaspoons palm
  sugar/jaggery
½ teaspoon garam
  masala
freshly squeezed juice
  of ½ lemon, plus
  wedges to serve
2 tablespoons freshly
  chopped coriander/
  cilantro
naan bread, to serve

SERVES 8

This black chickpea and tomato curry makes a great vegetarian option. I use black chickpeas here because they have a more nutty and intense flavour than regular white chickpeas. The sauce is generally quite thin – almost broth-like – and the flavour is enhanced with fresh curry leaves and holy trinity paste.

Heat the oil in a heavy-bottomed pan over medium heat and add the cloves. Allow the oil to become infused with warm aromatic notes of the cloves. Next, add the mustard seeds and allow them to sizzle in the pan. Add the cumin and fenugreek seeds and allow them to sizzle and crackle. The seeds are ready when they start popping and releasing their aromatic oils.

Add the ginger and garlic to the pan and allow them to become golden-brown, then add the fresh curry leaves. Take care as they will splutter in the hot oil. Add the onions and salt and fry until soft, browned and caramelized, stirring often. This will take a good 20–25 minutes.

Add the holy trinity paste, mix well with the onions and fry for 2 minutes.

We have now started to layer our flavours (see page 10). Next, add the turmeric, cumin, coriander and paprika to the pan and mix well. It is important to cook out spices, because if they remain raw, your curry will have a harsh flavour, as well as a grainy texture. The ground spices will dry out your pan, so, to stop your pan from burning, add a splash of water to keep it moist (this will also help the spices to cook; I add about 100 ml/⅓ cup at this stage).

Add the tomato purée/paste and mix well. Add the tomatoes, stir well, reduce the heat to medium and put a lid on the pan. (You can use canned tomatoes if you prefer but, for this dish, I find them too sour and acidic.) You will know when the tomatoes are ready because the flesh will start to melt and the whole mix will come together nicely as a sauce; this takes 12–15 minutes.

Add the boiled onion purée for extra body and velvety mouthfeel, and cook for 6–7 minutes.

Add the chickpeas, mix well, then add the sugar and 200 ml/¾ cup of water. Allow to simmer, with the lid on, over medium heat for 5 minutes. To add the final dimensions to the flavour of this curry, add the garam masala, lemon juice and freshly chopped coriander/cilantro for a citrusy freshness.

Check the taste and consistency; saltiness and sweetness, and the looseness of the sauce.

Remove from the heat and serve with naan bread and lemon wedges.

CHICKPEA, KALE AND COCONUT KORMA

This korma is a prime example of modern Indian cuisine. It is nothing like what you would find in any Indian home or restaurant. Chickpeas are a staple Indian ingredient, kale is not. Coconut is a regional Indian ingredient, the korma is a dish which divides opinion. As a name, there is a lot of conflict with the concept of this dish, when cooked however, the ingredients dance together and create this truly magical recipe. Not only is it great for vegetarians, but meat-lovers tend to enjoy it too.

5 tablespoons vegetable oil
2 cloves
3 cardamom pods
½ teaspoon cumin seeds
2 large onions, finely diced
1 teaspoon salt
1 teaspoon Holy Trinity Paste (page 12)
1 teaspoon ground cumin
1 teaspoon ground coriander
1 teaspoon ground turmeric
1 teaspoon tomato purée/paste
3 tablespoons ground almonds
2 tablespoons unsweetened desiccated/shredded dried coconut
1 teaspoon caster/granulated sugar
200 ml/¾ cup coconut milk
240 g/1¾ cups drained canned chickpeas
100 g/3½ oz. kale, chopped and tough stalks removed
1 teaspoon garam masala
naan bread or cooked rice, to serve

SERVES 4

Heat the vegetable oil in a heavy-bottomed pan over medium heat, add the cloves and cardamom pods and allow to heat until you can see the spices sizzling. Add the cumin seeds and allow them to sizzle and crackle in the pan.

Add the onions and salt and fry until softened. This will take a good 25–30 minutes; it is best to cover the onions with a lid to prevent browning.

When the onions are completely softened and buttery, add the holy trinity paste and cook through until they no longer smell raw. Add the ground spices and mix well. If the pan is starting to dry out, add a splash of water to loosen the mix. Cook the spices out for a good 3–5 minutes.

Next, add the tomato purée/paste and mix well. Again, if the pan is drying out, add another splash of water. Once the tomato purée/paste is completely mixed in with the other ingredients, add the ground almonds, unsweetened desiccated/shredded dried coconut and sugar, and mix well. Pour in 200 ml/¾ cup of water to make the 'base' of your korma sauce. Add the coconut milk, mix well and leave to simmer for a good 3–4 minutes. Add the chickpeas, mix well and leave to simmer for 3 minutes. Add the kale and stir into the sauce for 1 minute. Sprinkle over the garam masala, stir in and remove from the heat.

Serve with naan bread or rice.

STIR-FRY BINDHI

Growing up, I hated okra/ladies' fingers; I always remember it being slimy with a soft, mushy texture that I could never seem to take to. Over the years, when experimenting with recipes, I found a way to make it more appealing. Here, I have created a recipe where the okra/ladies' fingers is stir-fried, which means it retains its natural flavour and texture. It is fried in a cumin and mustard seed-infused oil which creates an earthy base. Garlic and ginger is used to enhance the freshness of the dish, while black salt and mango powder are added right at the end to create a combination of a sulphurous and acidic flavour.

500 g/1 lb. 2 oz. okra/ ladies' fingers
4 tablespoons vegetable oil
1 teaspoon mustard seeds
1 teaspoon cumin seeds
1 teaspoon fine julienne of fresh root ginger
2 garlic cloves, thinly sliced
¼ teaspoon ajwain seeds
½ teaspoon salt
¼ teaspoon black salt
½ teaspoon mango powder (sometimes called 'amchoor powder')
¼ teaspoon dried chilli/ hot red pepper flakes

SERVES 4
AS AN ACCOMPANIMENT

Rinse and dry the okra/ladies' fingers, then cut in half lengthways. (Frying wet okra/ladies' fingers often creates a sticky texture causing an unpleasant mouthfeel, so dry them well.)

Heat the vegetable oil in a large wok over medium heat. Add the mustard seeds and allow to sizzle, then add the cumin seeds and fry until they have popped.

Add the ginger and garlic and fry in the oil until they become slightly browned. Add the ajwain seeds and toss in the hot oil for 30 seconds. Add the okra/ladies' fingers, the two types of salt, the mango powder and dried chilli/hot red pepper flakes, and toss around to cover the okra/ladies' fingers in the seasoned oil and spices. Fry until softened and the sticky substance that is released from cutting the flesh disappears. Cover the pan with a lid to help soften the okra/ladies' fingers if necessary; it should take no longer than 15–20 minutes to cook.

Serve as a side dish.

VEG MANCHURIAN

In India, there is a growing trend towards Indian and Chinese fusion dishes. India and China are next to each other geographically and share the same border, so naturally there will be some crossover regarding food. This dish is an Indian take on Chinese cuisine and is served to Indian diners who want to experience 'traditional' Chinese cooking. The vegetable fritters are deep-fried and served in a reduced spicy and salty sauce.

FRITTERS
- 145 g/generous 1 cup grated carrot
- 145 g/generous 2 cups shredded white cabbage
- 60 g/scant 1 cup sliced spring onions/scallions
- 80 g/½ cup thinly sliced green/French beans
- 1 teaspoon Holy Trinity Paste (page 12)
- 3 tablespoons plain/all-purpose flour
- 2 tablespoons cornflour/cornstarch
- ½ teaspoon salt
- vegetable oil, for deep-frying

SAUCE
- 4 tablespoons vegetable oil
- 1 teaspoon finely diced fresh root ginger
- 1 teaspoon finely diced garlic
- 100 ml/⅓ cup light soy sauce
- 100 ml/⅓ cup vegetable stock
- 50 ml/3½ tablespoons red chilli/chili sauce
- 2 teaspoons cornflour/cornstarch
- 1 green chilli/chile, thinly sliced
- 2 spring onions/scallions, sliced, to garnish

deep-fat fryer (optional)

SERVES 4

Mix together all of the ingredients to make the vegetable fritters (apart from the oil for frying) in a large mixing bowl. When all of the mixture has come together, form it into even balls (around the same size as a golf ball). You may want to do this in batches, as the fritters fry best when freshly rolled.

Heat the vegetable oil in a deep-fat fryer or large, heavy-bottomed pan to 180°C (350°F). Carefully add the fritters, in batches, and deep-fry each batch for 5–6 minutes each until golden-brown. Drain on paper towels to absorb any excess oil and set aside until required.

For the sauce, heat the vegetable oil in a wok or a saucepan over low–medium heat and fry the ginger and garlic until golden-brown. Add the soy sauce, vegetable stock, 400 ml/1⅔ cups of water and the chilli/chili sauce and allow to gently come up to the boil.

Mix the cornflour/cornstarch with a splash of cold water and add to the pan. Allow the sauce to thicken slightly and simmer for 2 minutes, stirring occasionally.

Add the fried fritter balls to the sauce and gently mix in, being careful not to break any of the fritters. Sprinkle over the green chilli/chile and spring onion/scallion slices, and serve.

SAMBHARO

Sambharo is a traditional Gujarati vegetarian side dish. It is shredded cabbage and carrot which is stir-fried in a seasoned oil that is flavoured with pungent seeds, spices, chillies/chiles and fresh curry leaves. The recipe is super-simple to make and is a great replacement for any slaw. I enjoy this dish on its own or alongside any other curry.

4 tablespoons vegetable oil
1 teaspoon mustard seeds
1 teaspoon cumin seeds
½ teaspoon fenugreek seeds
1 teaspoon finely diced fresh root ginger
½ teaspoon finely diced garlic
1 teaspoon fennel seeds
4 green chillies/chiles, slit
25 fresh curry leaves
350 g/2½ cups shredded carrot
425 g/6¾ cups grated cabbage
1½ teaspoons salt, or to taste
Naani Maa's Lemon Pickle (page 130), to serve

SERVES 4

Heat the oil in a heavy-bottomed pan over medium heat and add the mustard seeds. When they start to sizzle, add the cumin seeds and fenugreek seeds until they crackle and pop. Add the diced ginger and garlic and fry until they become golden-brown.

Add the fennel seeds, chillies/chiles and curry leaves, and mix the whole lot together in the pan. This spiced oil is the main carrier of flavour for the whole dish.

Add the carrot and cabbage and mix well so that the oil coats all of the veg. Because this is a stir-fry dish (and can be eaten as a salad or slaw), you don't want to overcook the carrot or cabbage. I keep the pan over medium heat for about 6 minutes, so the veg still has a crunch to it.

Season with salt to taste, then serve with Naani Maa's lemon pickle.

KICKIN' CAULIFLOWER

Despite cauliflower now being a staple ingredient all over India, the versatile vegetable does not actually originate from India. In fact, cauliflower has only been in cultivation in India for the last 200 years and was introduced to the county by the British during the British Raj as a way 'to recreate a sense of belonging for the colonisers in the colony'. Having once taken centre stage on elaborate European dinner tables, it didn't take long for the humble cauliflower (gobi), to be used as a main ingredient for family favourite recipes such as Aloo Gobi or Gobi Paratha. Despite being super simple, this dish makes a great accompaniment to spice up a roast dinner or even to be enjoyed as a snack on its own. To complement the natural, sweet, nuttiness of the cauliflower I have created a Tandoori-style marinade which gives it quite a kick!

800 g/10²/₃ cups cauliflower florets (about 1 large cauliflower)
freshly chopped coriander/cilantro, to garnish

MARINADE
2 tablespoons natural/plain yogurt
20 fresh curry leaves
1 teaspoon garlic purée
1 teaspoon ginger purée
2 teaspoons salt
2 tablespoons vegetable oil
1 teaspoon dried fenugreek leaves
1 teaspoon cumin seeds
1 teaspoon coriander seeds
1 teaspoon mustard seeds
1 teaspoon dried chilli/hot red pepper flakes
1 tablespoon gram/chickpea flour
1 teaspoon ground turmeric
freshly squeezed juice of ½ lemon

baking sheet, lined with baking parchment

SERVES 5

Preheat the oven to 180°C (350°F) Gas 4.

Bring a pan of salted water to the boil and add the cauliflower florets. Boil for 3–4 minutes, but no more as you don't want to overcook them. Drain in a colander and leave to stand in the colander to allow all of the excess water to evaporate.

Meanwhile, combine all of the marinade ingredients with 2 tablespoons of water. Add the blanched cauliflower florets and mix really well. This is quite a thin marinade, which allows it to get into all of the nooks and crannies of the cauliflower florets. Don't be alarmed by the excess water in the bottom of the bowl as this well help cook the cauliflower without it drying out in the oven.

Spread the marinated cauliflower out on the prepared baking sheet. Roast in the preheated oven for 25–30 minutes, stirring every 10 minutes to ensure that the florets do not start to burn.

Once the cauliflower has cooked through (I like to keep a little bite to the florets), remove from the oven, sprinkle over the freshly chopped coriander/cilantro and serve.

ROASTED PILI PILI MOGO CHIPS

1 kg/2¼ lbs. frozen cassava, peeled and wedged (available in most large supermarkets)

SPICE MIX
5 tablespoons vegetable oil
1 teaspoon rock salt
1 teaspoon dried chilli/ hot red pepper flakes
1 teaspoon crushed coriander seeds
1 teaspoon cumin seeds
½ teaspoon crushed black pepper
1 teaspoon finely diced garlic
1 teaspoon finely diced ginger

TAMARIND SAUCE
180 g/¾ cup tamarind paste
50 g/¼ cup demerara/ turbinado sugar
1 teaspoon paprika

SERVES 4–5
AS A SNACK

A lot of the food that I eat is actually based upon east African recipes and ingredients, one of them being cassava or 'mogo', which is a woody, starchy root vegetable. It's a great replacement for potato and takes on a lot of flavour. Unlike normal potato chips/fries, mogo holds its form well and retains a great texture for a good few days, which is why it can be used to make such a great snack on the go. This recipe means a lot to me because the first time I made it for my parents, my mother said with excitement 'this tastes exactly like the mogo chips I used to buy from the stalls outside my school in Uganda!' The generic 'peri-peri' sauce, originally called 'pili-pili' is the Swahili expression for 'pepper pepper'. For this recipe, I developed a spicy and aromatic spice mix to create a depth of flavour, and also a tamarind sauce to add a fresh sweet and sour element to the dish.

Preheat the oven to 170°C (325°F) Gas 3.

Put the cassava wedges in a pan of boiling water and cook for 10–12 minutes. Drain away the water and let the wedges sit in a colander to steam in the remaining heat.

Combine all of the ingredients for the spice mix in a bowl. Stir well to create a paste and scrape onto a baking sheet. Spread the paste out evenly and roast in the preheated oven for 2–3 minutes. Add the cassava to the baking sheet and toss well so that the wedges are well coated in the spice mix. Roast the cassava for 12–15 minutes or until they become golden-brown. Keep turning them around during cooking to prevent them from burning, and add a little drizzle of oil if the mix gets too dry.

While the cassava is roasting, make your tamarind sauce. Place the tamarind paste, sugar, paprika and 50 ml/3½ tablespoons of water in a pan and gently simmer for 5–6 minutes until everything comes together to a sauce.

Remove the roasted cassava from the oven and drizzle over 3 tablespoons of the tamarind sauce. Toss around to coat. Serve on a plate with the remaining tamarind sauce in a separate dipping pot to accompany.

Note If you can't find concentrated tamarind paste, you can make your own by soaking a dried 200 g/7 oz. slab of tamarind in hot water for 30 minutes, mixing well with your hands to loosen up the fruit and passing it through a fine-mesh sieve/strainer.

RICE, CHUTNEY AND RAITA

The world is a big place and with tourism on the rise, people are better-travelled than they have ever been. I'm often asked by my friends, family and colleagues about new and interesting Indian dishes they have tried when out and about – they want to know about the origins of a recipe, to learn the 'story' behind the dish. Not only do they want to taste great food, they also want to be educated about it.

Indian food is all about the meal experience and this means the meal has to deliver in appearance, aroma and texture, as well as taste. One thing I have learnt over the years is that it is okay to achieve this through the addition of various 'mini' dishes. No Indian meal is complete without its accompaniments; the central dish acts as the 'body' of a meal delivering the main flavours, most often a curry. With a curry you need either a bread or rice dish to act as the carrier or 'legs', which soaks up the sauce. To take a meal to the next level you will often see Indian dishes served with a pickle, chutney or a yogurt-based dip such as raita (my Tomato, Cucumber and Mint Raita on page 130 is sumptuously creamy!).

These types of dishes, often served cold, help to add a different dimension to the meal, be that by adding to the texture or taste by adding spice or sourness, cooling the heat of the main dish, or adding to it. They tell the story of the central dish and are essential for creating well-balanced Indian meals. The recipes in this chapter demonstrate how accompanying rice dishes vary in regards to cooking processes and simplicity. It also showcases a beautiful variety of dips in the form of pickles, chutneys and raitas, which can be eaten alongside any Indian main course or entrée.

A note to all you pickle-lovers, my grandmother's Naani Maa's Lemon Pickle on page 130 is to die for! You only need one or two pieces of lemon to complete your meal, but I couldn't do without it.

MUSHROOM PILAU

Now this is a dish that you will likely find in every Indian curry house and it's somewhat of a guilty pleasure of mine if I'm honest. Mushrooms aren't widely used in Indian cuisine, but when they are, great things are possible! I like to cook with mushrooms because the texture can be quite meaty and the flavour they release is rather savoury and umami. This is a lovely, simple, little dish, but it certainly delivers on flavour. You can use any type of mushroom you like – I use a mix of shiitake, chestnut and white mushrooms.

4 tablespoons vegetable oil
1 teaspoon cumin seeds
2 garlic cloves, finely diced
4 shiitake mushrooms, cut into 5-mm/ ¼-inch slices (about 70 g/½ cup)
8 chestnut mushrooms, cut into 5-mm/ ¼-inch slices (about 120 g/1 cup)
8 closed cup white mushrooms, cut into 5-mm/¼-inch slices (about 120 g/1 cup)

1 teaspoon paprika
1 teaspoon salt
½ teaspoon cracked black pepper
500 g/scant 3 cups basmati rice (rinsed)
2 tablespoons ghee
1 tablespoon freshly chopped coriander/ cilantro

SERVES 5

Heat the vegetable oil in a heavy-bottomed pan over medium heat and fry the cumin seeds until they crackle and pop. Add the garlic and fry until lightly browned. Add all the sliced mushrooms and fry for 5–6 minutes until cooked. Stir occasionally to prevent them from sticking to the bottom of the pan.

Add the paprika, salt and pepper and mix well.

Add the rice and mix well so that the mushrooms and rice are evenly distributed.

Pour over 750 ml/3 cups of water and gently bring to the boil. Once the water starts to boil, reduce the heat to low, cover the pan with a lid and simmer gently for 10 minutes.

Once the rice grains are fully cooked but still retain a little bite, remove the pan from the heat and set aside with the lid on for 6–8 minutes, so that the grains continue to steam and puff up nicely in the pan.

Add the ghee, mix well to cover the rice grains, then sprinkle over the freshly chopped coriander/ cilantro and serve.

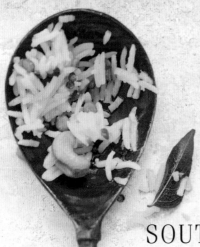

SOUTH INDIAN RICE

South Indian-style rice makes a great accompaniment to dishes in place of plain boiled rice. The seasoned oil creates a wonderful aromatic depth of flavour that is carried through every mouthful. This dish has a nuttiness from the fried lentils, a savouriness from the mustard seeds and curry leaves, a spice kick from the chilli/chile and a rich sweetness from the coconut milk.

200 g/1 cup plus 2 tablespoons basmati rice (rinsed)

50 ml/3½ tablespoons coconut milk

4 tablespoons vegetable oil

1 teaspoon channa dhal

1 teaspoon urad dhal

1 teaspoon mustard seeds

6–8 cashew nuts

1 dried red chilli/chile

12 large fresh curry leaves

SERVES 5

Boil the rice in 600 ml/2½ cups of water until it is three-quarters cooked and the water has nearly all been absorbed. Add the coconut milk and stir in well. Cover the pan with a lid, remove from the heat and leave to stand. The rice will continue to cook in the steam in the pan.

Heat the oil in a small wok over a low–medium heat, add the channa dhal and urad dal and move them around in the pan until they become golden-brown.

Add the mustard seeds and allow them to crackle. Remove the pan from the heat when the seeds have popped.

Add the cashew nuts, chilli/chile and curry leaves to the hot seeded oil and mix well. Be careful when adding the curry leaves as they will splutter and the oil will be very hot.

Pour the seasoned oil over the rice and serve.

KEDGEREE

Kedgeree is a dish which boasts many years of tradition, fusion and cultural history. It symbolizes colonial India and dates back to the reign of Queen Victoria, created by one of her personal chefs for Florence Nightingale. As a child I grew up eating a dish called 'kichdi' for breakfast which is a soft-cooked, curried, rice dish. It was only once I trained as a chef that I learnt that kedgeree is actually a take on kichdi but with the addition of smoked haddock and eggs.

350 g/12 oz. undyed smoked haddock fillets

2 bay leaves

6 peppercorns

2 UK large/US extra-large eggs

4 tablespoons vegetable oil

1 teaspoon mustard seeds

1 teaspoon cumin seeds

15 fresh curry leaves

1 onion, finely chopped

1 teaspoon salt

1 teaspoon Holy Trinity Paste (page 12)

1 teaspoon ground turmeric

2 teaspoons curry powder

2 tablespoons tomato purée/paste

200 g/7 oz. canned chopped tomatoes

370 g/2 cups basmati rice (rinsed)

3 tablespoons single/light cream

freshly squeezed juice of 1 lemon

2 tablespoons freshly chopped coriander/cilantro

Put the smoked haddock fillets flat in a pan, skin-side down. Add the bay leaves and peppercorns and cover with cold water. Gently simmer over medium heat for 8–10 minutes. Drain and set aside to cool.

Bring a pan of water to the boil and gently lower in the eggs with a spoon. Boil for 7 minutes, then remove using a slotted spoon and place in a bowl of iced water. Leave them in the water to cool, then peel and set aside.

Heat the vegetable oil in a heavy-bottomed pan over medium heat, add the mustard and cumin seeds and allow to sizzle and crackle. Add the curry leaves and toss the pan slightly to infuse all of the flavours in the oil.

Add the onion and salt and stir well. Cook until the onion has become soft and golden-brown. Once the onion has softened, add the holy trinity paste. Fry until the raw aroma has disappeared. Add the turmeric and curry powder, stir well and cook for 3–4 minutes. Add a splash of water if the pan gets too dry.

Add the tomato purée/paste to the pan and fry out for 1 minute. Add the chopped tomatoes and mix well in the pan. Gently simmer the sauce base for 3–4 minutes.

Add the rice and coat the grains well in the sauce mix. Add 1 litre/quart of water and bring to the boil, then reduce to low heat, place a lid on top and simmer for 10 minutes.

Remove from the heat and set aside, covered with the lid, for 10 minutes. The excess water in the pan will steam and be absorbed by the rice. I prefer this method of absorption for cooking rice rather than boiling the rice because it gives the grains a better texture.

Once all of the water has been absorbed and the rice is cooked, add the cream and lemon juice and stir well until the rice is all coated.

Remove the skin from the haddock and gently flake the fish into big bite-sized chunks. Peel and quarter the eggs. Add the haddock flakes and egg quarters into the rice mix and gently fold in.

Sprinkle over the freshly chopped coriander/cilantro and serve.

SERVES 5

CHICKEN BIRIYANI

Biriyani is something of a national dish in India, but it varies according to region, family recipe, diet and the likes and dislikes of a particular chef. This recipe is an everyday one unlike the Gosht Dum Biriyani (pages 90–91), which is more of a celebratory dish. It uses chicken, which is a much cheaper meat than lamb, and is a one-pot recipe that requires very little preparation other than marinating the chicken. I find that using chicken on the bone delivers an intense flavour, but boneless chicken can be used too, simply cook for less time.

1 kg/2¼ lbs. chicken on the bone, portioned into pieces

MARINADE
1 tablespoon vegetable oil
1 tablespoon Holy Trinity Paste (page 12)
1 teaspoon Kashmiri chilli/chili powder
1 teaspoon paprika
1½ teaspoons ground coriander
1½ teaspoons ground cumin
1 teaspoon garam masala
2 tablespoons natural/plain yogurt
2 teaspoons salt

RICE MIX
4 tablespoons vegetable oil
1 tablespoon fine julienne of fresh root ginger
6 cloves
a 7.5-cm/3-inch cinnamon stick
6 cardamom pods
1 teaspoon cumin seeds
2 bay leaves
1 onion, finely chopped
1 teaspoon salt
3 large tomatoes, peeled and finely chopped (core and seeds removed)
500 g/scant 3 cups basmati rice (rinsed)

TO SERVE
Crispy Fried Onions (page 12)
Tomato, Cucumber and Mint Raita (page 130)

SERVES 6

Combine all of the marinade ingredients together in a mixing bowl, add the chicken and mix well. Allow the chicken to marinate overnight for best results. If you do not have time, you can leave it for a minimum of 30 minutes at room temperature.

To prepare the rice mix, heat the oil in a heavy-bottomed pan over low heat and fry the ginger until golden-brown. Add the cloves, cinnamon stick and cardamom pods and fry for 30 seconds until the spices release their aromatic oils and fragrances. Add the cumin seeds and allow to sizzle, then add the bay leaves and toss in the hot oil.

Add the onion and salt and mix well. Fry until softened and golden-brown, covering with a lid to help the onion to soften. If the pan dries out too much, add a drizzle of oil.

Add the tomatoes then the marinated chicken and mix well to coat in the spices and seal. Fry the chicken with the onion mix for 35 minutes until cooked and tender.

Add the rice, mix well for 2 minutes, then pour in 1 litre/quart of water. Stir to mix well. Allow the water to come up to the boil, then reduce the heat to low and cover with a lid. Cook the biriyani for 12 minutes.

Keep the biriyani covered with a lid, remove it from the heat and allow to stand for 5–8 minutes. The rice grains should puff up in the excess steam. Serve with crispy fried onions.

GOAN SAUSAGE AND KING PRAWN/ JUMBO SHRIMP PILAF

This recipe is a cross between two traditional rice dishes; a paella and an Indian pilaf. It highlights the Mediterranean influence that the Portuguese explorers had in India, in particular Goa. Because of the large Christian population, pork is eaten more in Goa than in any other part of India, and, as a result, the Goan people have created some wonderful pork-based products, staying true to their Indian roots. One product which I'm very fond of in particular, is the Goan sausage which is very similar to a chorizo-style sausage but heavily flavoured with fresh chillies/chiles and garam masala. Unlike any other traditional Indian rice dish, this one includes different types of protein; mixing seafood and meat together while still keeping the rice mix itself very flavoursome and fragrant. (Pictured pages 128–129)

CHICKEN THIGHS
4 boneless, skinless chicken thighs, cut into 2.5-cm/1-inch cubes
2 tablespoons vegetable oil
½ teaspoon salt
½ teaspoon crushed black pepper
½ teaspoon chilli/chili powder

KING PRAWNS/ JUMBO SHRIMP
12 fresh raw king prawns/jumbo shrimp (heads and shells left on)
1 tablespoon vegetable oil
½ teaspoon paprika
freshly squeezed juice of ½ lime

RICE MIX
3 tablespoons vegetable oil
3 cardamom pods
3 cloves
a 5-cm/2-inch cinnamon stick
1 teaspoon cumin seeds
2 garlic cloves, finely diced
100 g/3½ oz. Goan sausage, diced
1 large onion, finely chopped
1 teaspoon salt
1 teaspoon ground turmeric
1 teaspoon chilli/chili powder
1 teaspoon ground cumin
1 teaspoon ground coriander

a pinch of saffron strands, steeped in a little warm water
1 tablespoon tomato purée/paste
200 g/7 oz. canned chopped tomatoes
1 red (bell) pepper, deseeded and diced
300 g/1¾ cups basmati rice (rinsed)
100 g/⅔ cup frozen peas, defrosted
freshly squeezed juice of 1 lemon

TO FINISH
sliced red (bell) pepper
freshly chopped coriander/cilantro

SERVES 8

Combine all of the ingredients for the chicken thighs together in a mixing bowl. Mix well to coat the meat and set aside to marinate. (It is not crucial that the chicken has an overnight marinade; 30 minutes at room temperature will be fine.)

In another mixing bowl, combine the ingredients for the king prawns/jumbo shrimp and put in the refrigerator to marinate for 30 minutes.

Once the chicken and prawns are marinated, they need to be sealed so that they are ready to go into the pilaf and are not completely raw. Set a large frying pan/skillet or paellera over medium heat, add the marinated chicken and seal well. Remove from the pan and set aside on a plate. Leave any excess oil and juices in the pan. Add the prawns/shrimp to the pan and fry on each side for no longer than 20 seconds. (All you want to do is change the colour of the shell from grey to red – they will fully cook towards the end of this recipe.) Remove the prawns/shrimp from the pan and set aside. Pour all of the excess oil and juices into another pan where you will cook the rice mix next. (You can still use your paellera to serve your dish.)

Heat the oil in this pan and add the cardamom pods, cloves and cinnamon stick. Fry in the oil for 30 seconds to release the aromatic flavours from the spices. Add the cumin seeds, toss in the oil and fry for 30 seconds or until the seeds start to sizzle. Add the garlic and lightly brown.

Next, fry the Goan sausage with the spices and allow to seal on all edges. Keep tossing in the hot oil to prevent it from sticking to the pan.

Add the onion and salt, mix well and allow to soften and brown.

Next, add the turmeric, chilli/chili powder, cumin and ground coriander, and the saffron steeped in warm water. Mix really well with the onions and cook until the raw aroma has disappeared. If the pan is becoming too dry, add a splash of water.

Add the tomato purée/paste, stir and coat all of the ingredients in the pan well. Warm through for 5 minutes, then add the canned tomatoes. Mix well and gently simmer for 2 minutes.

Add the sealed chicken and diced red (bell) pepper, mix well and gently simmer for 12–15 minutes or until the chicken is cooked through.

Add the basmati rice and stir well to coat the grains in the tomato sauce. Pour in 750 ml/3 cups of water to cover. Reduce the heat and allow the rice to come up to a gentle boil. Once the water starts to boil, place a lid on the pan and cook over very low heat for 8–10 minutes or until the rice grains are almost cooked through.

Add the peas and lemon juice, stir well, remove from the heat and cover with a lid. Allow to rest for 8–10 minutes. The rice grains will finish cooking in the excess steam.

When the rice is fully cooked, start to assemble your dish. A pilaf is a wonderful sharing dish, so I like to serve it as one large dish, however, if your pan or paellera is not large enough, you can serve an assembled portion per person.

Spread the cooked rice mix out in your paellera (or the frying pan/skillet you used earlier). Do not do this too evenly, as you want it to look quite rustic. Add the fried prawns/shrimp and the red (bell) pepper slices. Cover with a lid (or foil if you do not have a lid big enough) and return to low heat for 1–2 minutes to allow the prawns/shrimp to finish cooking. Keep stirring around to prevent the rice sticking to the bottom and burning. Sprinkle over the freshly chopped coriander/cilantro and serve immediately.

NAANI MAA'S LEMON PICKLE

As I have mentioned throughout this book, I owe a lot to my grandmother for the cooking techniques and recipes she has taught me. One recipe in particular, which she has nailed, is this lemon pickle.

500 g/1 lb. 2 oz. lemons
4 teaspoons rock salt
1 teaspoon ground turmeric
2 teaspoons chilli/chili powder
1 teaspoon ground coriander
1 teaspoon ground cumin
1 teaspoon ground ginger
3 tablespoons vegetable oil
a 5-cm/2-inch cinnamon stick
1 teaspoon cumin seeds
1 teaspoon fennel seeds
500 g/2½ cups palm sugar/jaggery

a sterilized glass jar fitted with an airtight lid

SERVES 16

Bring a pan of water to the boil. Add the lemons and boil them whole for 8–10 minutes or until soft, then drain. Cut each lemon into eight equal wedges and put them in a large mixing bowl (adding all the excess lemon juice as well). Sprinkle over the salt, turmeric, chilli/chili powder, ground coriander, cumin and ginger. Mix well.

Heat the oil in a heavy-bottomed pan over medium heat, add the cinnamon stick and cumin seeds and allow to sizzle and crackle. Add the fennel seeds and toss in the hot oil for 20 seconds. Pour this over the lemons and mix well. Set aside.

Add the palm sugar/jaggery and 3 tablespoons of water to a separate pan and mix well. Set over a low heat and allow the sugar to melt slowly.

Once the sugar has become a syrup, add the marinated lemon wedges along with the seasoned oil and any excess juices which may have been released. Mix well and simmer gently for 2 minutes. Do not allow the lemons to boil as the pickle will become bitter.

Store the lemon pickle in the sterilized glass jar fitted with an airtight lid. It should last for up to 3 months at room temperature – once opened, store in the refrigerator for up to 2 weeks.

TOMATO, CUCUMBER AND MINT RAITA

Yogurt is a huge part of Indian cuisine and raita, a flavoured yogurt dip, is often served as an accompaniment to 'cool down' the palate but to also complement and enhance another dish. Raita, like most other Indian dips, varies in style. The recipe below is the one that I have used for years and has never let me down. It is very simple which is great for when you are making a meal in a hurry.

1 teaspoon cumin seeds
500 ml/2 cups natural/plain yogurt
1 large tomato, finely chopped (core and seeds removed)
½ cucumber, grated 6 large mint leaves, finely chopped, plus extra to garnish
1 teaspoon salt
1 teaspoon caster/granulated sugar
a pinch of chilli/chili powder

SERVES 4

Toast the cumin seeds in a dry frying pan/skillet until they darken and become aromatic with an earthy fragrance. Pound the seeds using a pestle and mortar to form a powder and set aside.

Whisk the yogurt in a large mixing bowl until smooth. Add all the remaining ingredients, including the ground cumin, check the seasoning and serve, garnished with fresh mint. Store in the refrigerator if not required straight away.

MANGO AND CHILLI/CHILE SALSA

This recipe is one of my modern classics. Ripe mangos are not usually eaten in savoury dishes in India, but having taken inspiration from other cultures, including the Caribbean, I think the mango and chilli/chile, together with the red onion, vinegar, sugar and blend of spices all work together beautifully to deliver a fresh, zingy, colourful, sweet, sour and hugely addictive salsa. It goes with pretty much every dish. (Pictured page 133)

3 tablespoons white wine vinegar

2 tablespoons demerara/turbinado sugar

1 large mango, peeled, stoned/pitted and finely diced

1 large red onion, finely diced

4 red chillies/chiles (preferably sweet not spicy), finely diced

1 green chilli/chile, finely diced

a medium bunch of coriander/cilantro, freshly chopped

3 tomatoes, finely chopped (core and seeds removed)

½ teaspoon salt

½ teaspoon crushed black pepper

15 mint leaves, finely chopped

SERVES 5

Put the vinegar and brown sugar in a pan and heat gently together until the sugar has dissolved. Set the pan aside and leave to cool.

Put the remaining ingredients (except the chopped mint leaves) in a mixing bowl and mix.

Add the chopped mint leaves to the chilled vinegar and sugar mixture and stir well to infuse the mint flavours into the reduction.

Stir the reduction into the mixing bowl and leave to stand for 10 minutes. Check the seasoning of the salsa and serve.

TAMARIND CHUTNEY

Tamarind is a fruit which is both sweet and sour in taste and therefore provides the perfect base ingredient for a chutney. This recipe makes a delicious accompaniment to the majority of snacks, it is fresh, rich, zingy and explosive in flavour. I always have a store of tamarind chutney in my fridge ready to eat alongside samosas, chicken wings and even chips/fries.

180 g/¾ cup tamarind paste (see Note)

50 g/¼ cup demerara/turbinado sugar

1 teaspoon paprika

SERVES 4

Put the tamarind paste, paprika, sugar and 50 ml/3½ tablespoons of water in a saucepan and gently simmer over low heat for 10–12 minutes until the ingredients come together a syrupy sauce. Remove from the heat, cool to room temperature, then chill.

Store in the refrigerator for up to 1 week if not required straight away.

Note If you can't find concentrated tamarind paste, you can make your own by soaking a dried 200 g/7 oz. slab of tamarind in hot water for 30 minutes, mixing well with your hands to loosen up the fruit and passing through a fine-mesh sieve/strainer.

HARIYALI CHUTNEY

I sometimes refer to this chutney as my 'jungle chutney' because of its gorgeous, bright, striking green colour. It has more recently been a success amongst friends and family because it ties in with the whole 'green juice' trend of healthy foodies. And I'm pleased to say it is actually quite healthy, because it is raw and so all of the natural vitamins and other nutrients from the fresh coriander/cilantro and mint are not cooked away. The flavour is incredibly fresh and refreshing, it's boosted with citrusy lime and finished off with earthy toasted cumin seeds. (Pictured page 132, right)

100 g/2 cups freshly chopped coriander/cilantro (leaves and stalks)

35 g/1¼ cups freshly chopped large mint leaves

2 green chillies/chiles

freshly squeezed juice of 1½ limes

1 teaspoon salt

2 heaped teaspoons unsweetened desiccated/dried shredded coconut

a 1.5-cm/½-inch squared piece of fresh root ginger

1 tablespoon natural/plain yogurt

1 teaspoon caster/granulated sugar

4 tablespoons vegetable oil

1 teaspoon cumin seeds, toasted

SERVES 5

Place all of the ingredients, except the toasted cumin seeds, in a food processor or blender and blitz together to make a chutney. Add the toasted cumin seeds, mix well and serve.

Store in the refrigerator if not required straight away.

COCONUT CHUTNEY

A celebration of south Indian ingredients – the nuttiness of the coconut is enhanced with explosive spices. (Pictured page 132, left)

CHUTNEY BASE

freshly grated flesh of 1 coconut

100 g/1⅓ cups unsweetened desiccated/dried shredded coconut

1 tablespoon channa dhal, toasted

1 green chilli/chile

a 1.5-cm/½-inch squared piece of fresh root ginger

1 teaspoon salt

300ml/1¼ cups water

SEASONED OIL

2 tablespoons vegetable oil

1 teaspoon urad dhal

½ teaspoon mustard seeds

½ teaspoon cumin seeds

½ teaspoon chilli/chili powder

10 fresh curry leaves

a pinch of asafoetida

TO FINISH

freshly squeezed juice of 1 lime

SERVES 6

Put all the ingredients for the chutney base in a tall measuring jug/cup and blitz together using a stick blender. Set aside until required.

Next, prepare the seasoned oil. Heat the oil in a pan over medium heat and add the urad dhal and mustard seeds and allow the mustard seeds to sizzle and crackle in the hot oil.

Next, add the cumin seeds and allow to pop. Add the chilli/chili powder, curry leaves and asafoetida and toss around well in the hot oil.

Pour the seasoned oil over the coconut chutney base while still hot, add the lime juice and stir well. Serve as an accompanying dip to any Indian starter or snack. This chutney is best eaten on the day on it's made as the coconut tends to soak up any excess water when left for a while.

DELIGHTFUL DESSERTS

A childhood memory I will always treasure is walking into Indian sweet shops with my mother and my nostrils filling up with the scent of sugar caramelizing that was emanating from the kitchen – Indian sweets being deep-fried, and milk slowly simmering away to form the base of so many tempting treats.

Across India, regional cuisines each have a plethora of different types of desserts. Some are eaten just for celebrations, some just at places of worship, but the majority of Indian desserts are, as with most other cuisines, eaten at the end of a meal.

People from India have a particularly sweet tooth. And why shouldn't they with India being the motherland of the humble sugar cane! I remember when touring Jaipur as a child, a lorry in front of our minibus had collapsed spilling tonnes of sugar cane across the pot-holed road. Our driver, like many others, dashed out of his seat and ran

back with his arms full of fresh sugar cane, which went down nicely as a treat during the course of the rest of the journey! As advised by my parents, you take a bite and chew the fibrous cane until there is no sugary liquid left – Mother Nature's chewing gum!

With the vast availability of sugar cane in India, the majority of desserts are heavily laced with sugar syrups, sprinkles, fillings and coatings. However, you will see that I have created a selection of desserts, which are a combination of both traditional Indian desserts and also my favourite desserts that I have mastered over the years of being a chef. I hope to take you on a journey which champions desserts, whether your favourite is the traditional Mango and Mint Kulfi on page 141, Pistachio Ice Cream on page 138, Chocolate and Madras Coffee Cake on page 157 or the classic panna cotta given a Darjeeling twist on page 150.

PISTACHIO ICE CREAM

Almost everyone I know loves ice cream and this dish is a perfect indulgence for serving at dinner parties. Pistachio nuts have always been associated with a high level of luxury and sophistication, and they work exceptionally well as a flavour profile for ice cream. I like to use chopped pistachio nuts as well as ground ones in order to add texture and a bit of a crunch to the smooth and soft ice cream.

285 ml/1¼ cups double/ heavy cream
285 ml/1¼ cups single/ light cream
75 g/generous ⅓ cup golden caster/ granulated sugar
40 g/generous ⅓ cup ground pistachio nuts
4 UK large/US extra- large egg yolks
1 tablespoon cornflour/ cornstarch
¼ teaspoon almond extract
20 g/⅙ cup coarsely chopped pistachio nuts

an ice-cream maker

SERVES 4
(MAKES 12 SCOOPS)

In a large mixing bowl, whisk the double/heavy cream until it is floppy but not stiff. Put in the refrigerator to keep cool.

Put the single/light cream in a pan with the sugar and ground pistachio nuts and gently heat to just below boiling point. Remove from the heat and set aside.

Beat the egg yolks, cornflour/cornstarch and almond extract together in another mixing bowl. Gently pour over the hot cream mixture, a little at a time, whisking well. Pour everything back into the pan and set over medium heat. Whisk until thickened to a custard.

Pour the hot custard into a clean mixing bowl, cover the surface with clingfilm/plastic wrap to prevent a skin from forming and put in the refrigerator to cool slightly.

After 15 minutes, check the temperature of the custard with your little finger. If the mix does not feel warm to your skin, then it is at the perfect temperature. Gently fold in the whisked double/heavy cream, being careful not to mix too hard (as this will make the cream lose its volume).

Gently mix in the chopped pistachio nuts. Pour the mixture into an ice-cream maker and churn for 30 minutes (or according to the manufacturer's instructions). Serve the ice cream alone or to accompany a warm dessert.

MANGO AND MINT KULFI

Kulfi is the Indian equivalent of ice cream and is a very popular and traditional dessert choice. It is meant to be denser, heavier and creamier than ice cream, which is why condensed milk is used, as it adds a lovely, rich and thick mouthfeel. This kulfi is great served all year round but eats exceptionally well during summer months as the combination of mango and mint make a tropical treat! I also use saffron in the recipe as it adds a warm fragrance.

3–4 saffron strands
500 ml/2 cups full-fat/ whole milk
100 ml/⅓ cup condensed milk
50 g/¼ cup caster/ granulated sugar
2 teaspoons cornflour/ cornstarch, dissolved in a little warm water
100 ml/⅓ cup double/ heavy cream
200 ml/¾ cup mango purée
15 large mint leaves, finely chopped, plus extra to serve

TO SERVE
chopped pistachio nuts
dried rose petals

SERVES 6

Soak the saffron strands in 2 tablespoons of the milk.

Meanwhile, pour the rest of the milk into a pan with the condensed milk and sugar, and gently bring to the boil. Simmer for 1 hour, stirring occasionally so that the mixture does not stick to the pan.

Once it has reduced by half, stir in the dissolved cornflour/cornstarch, ensuring that there are no lumps, and whisk into the hot kulfi mix. Simmer for 2 minutes, stirring occasionally and making sure that the mix does not stick to the pan. Add the double/heavy cream and saffron strands in milk. Mix in well.

Remove the pan from the heat and set aside to cool until the mix is no longer warm. Test with a clean finger.

Next, add the mango purée and the chopped mint and stir well to distribute the ingredients evenly. Transfer to a pouring jug/pitcher and pour into the desired serving dishes or moulds (I like to use traditional Indian clay pots to serve the kulfi in, but glass tumblers work well too). Freeze for 2–3 hours.

Serve straight from the freezer, sprinkled with extra mint, chopped pistachio nuts and dried rose petals for decoration.

ROSEWATER AND CARDAMOM GULAAB JAMUN

Gulaab Jamuns are an incredibly popular Indian treat. They are sweets, traditionally given out and eaten at special occasions. However, over the years, they have made it onto restaurant menus and become a popular dessert choice. The best way to describe a gulaab jamun is like a doughnut that has been soaked in syrup. The stock syrup is infused with cardamom pods and rosewater to create a fragrant scent and perfumed flavour.

80 g/1 cup milk powder (available in Indian grocery stores)
1½ tablespoons semolina
1½ tablespoons plain/ all-purpose flour
¼ teaspoon baking powder
1 tablespoon ghee, melted
1 teaspoon freshly squeezed lemon juice
50 ml/3½ tablespoons milk, warmed
vegetable oil, for deep-frying
dried rose petals, to serve

ROSEWATER SYRUP
1 teaspoon freshly squeezed lemon juice
250 g/1¼ cups caster/ granulated sugar
500 ml/2 cups water
1 teaspoon rosewater
4 cardamom pods, bruised
a pinch of saffron strands

deep-fat fryer (optional)

SERVES 4
(MAKES 16 BALLS)

Start by making the rosewater syrup. Put all of the ingredients in a pan and simmer over low heat for 10 minutes. Remove from the heat and set aside.

Heat the vegetable oil for deep-frying in a wok or deep-fat fryer to 180°C (350°F). Take care not to over-heat as the dough picks up colour almost instantly when fried.

Meanwhile, put the milk powder, semolina, flour and baking powder in a mixing bowl and mix well. Add the melted ghee and lemon juice and mix again. Drizzle in the warm milk, a little at a time, and mix well until the mixture forms a wet dough. Cover the bowl and set aside for 10 minutes.

Knead the dough well until smooth, making sure you get rid of any cracks.

Divide the dough into 16 equal pieces. Roll each piece in the palm of your hands to form a smooth ball with no cracks on the surface.

Deep-fry the balls, in batches, for 3–4 minutes, or until golden-brown and completely cooked through. Drain on paper towels. Transfer the warm balls to the rosewater syrup and return the pan to medium heat. Simmer for 2 minutes to gently warm everything together. Do not stir with a spoon as you can damage the balls; it's best to use the stick end of a wooden spoon. Sprinkle with dried rose petals and serve.

RASPBERRY RIPPLE AND ELDERFLOWER SHRIKAND

2 kg/4½ lbs. natural/
  plain yogurt
4 tablespoons caster/
  superfine sugar
¼ teaspoon ground
  cardamom

RIPPLE
250 g/9 oz. fresh
  raspberries
100 g/½ cup caster/
  granulated sugar
1 teaspoon cornflour/
  cornstarch
2 tablespoons water
2 tablespoons
  elderflower syrup (or
  elderflower cordial)

TO DECORATE
5–6 mint leaves
a handful of fresh
  raspberries

SERVES 5

Shrikand is a very traditional dessert that you may not have heard of before. This recipe, however, is by no means traditional! Shrikand is a celebration of the versatility of yogurt, simply hung to separate the curds from the whey and then flavoured. It has a texture and flavour like no other. The marriage of elderflower and raspberry works well to create a fragrant and sweet coulis that is perfect to marble into the shrikand base.

Line a fine sieve with a large piece of muslin/cheesecloth (a large, clean, thin tea towel will do too) place the lined sieve on a bowl so that it is securely balanced and place the yogurt into the centre of the muslin/cheesecloth. Bring in the corners of the cloth and a make a bundle/parcel of yoghurt. Tie the bundle/parcel together just above the yogurt with a large piece of kitchen string twine. The liquid collected in the bowl should not be touching the bottom of the sieve with the bundle in. Leave in the refrigerator overnight. (If there is no room in your refrigerator to do this, you can let the yogurt hang in a cold room for 2–3 hours.) You should be left with a ball of curd which looks similar to a mozzarella ball, and it should weigh about 700 g/1½ lbs.

Put the curd, sugar and ground cardamom in a bowl and whisk together until the sugar is no longer grainy. Put the mixing bowl in the refrigerator and let the mixture cool.

For the ripple, put the raspberries and sugar in a pan and gently simmer for 10 minutes or until the raspberries have melted into a coulis-like sauce. Dissolve the cornflour/cornstarch and water together, then add to the hot raspberry mixture and stir well. Simmer for 5–6 minutes to allow the mixture to thicken slightly. Remove from the heat and transfer to a bowl or container suitable for chilling. Put in the refrigerator and chill until completely cold. Mix in the elderflower syrup. Serve in bowls with ripple stirred through. Decorate with mint leaves and raspberries.

SAFFRON AND CARDAMOM KHEER

There is a certain nostalgia attached to this recipe. Kheer is an Indian rice pudding and rice pudding reminds me of my first school, so what better way to celebrate my childhood memories than to create my own recipe! I have mildly spiced my recipe with cardamom and cloves and flavoured the mix with saffron. It's a sweet, rich and creamy dessert that is incredibly comforting.

1.2 litres/quarts full-fat/
  whole milk, plus extra
  if needed
2 cardamom pods,
  crushed
2 cloves
a pinch of saffron
  strands

200 g/generous 1 cup
  pudding rice
50 g/¼ cup caster/
  granulated sugar
½ teaspoon ground
  cardamom

SERVES 6

Heat the milk, cardamom pods, cloves and saffron in a pan and gently bring to the boil. Stir in the pudding rice and gently simmer for 30 minutes.

Once the rice grains have softened, stir in the sugar and ground cardamom and simmer for a further 5 minutes. The thickness of this dessert completely depends on your preference – if you would like it thinner, simply add some more milk. Serve hot.

GAJJAR HALWA SAMOSAS

Samosas are a well-known Indian street food snack but the concept of pastry enclosing a filling is used all over the world. I wanted to take the idea and use it to create a traditional Indian dessert which is normally eaten on its own rather than as a filling. 'Gajjar halwa' is carrot that has been simmered in sweetened milk until the milk has reduced down. Pistachio nuts and raisins are added for sweetness, colour and texture. The gajjar halwa acts as a fantastic filling as it is quite robust which works well with the crispy fried pastry.

1 tablespoon ghee

700 g/5¼ cups grated carrot

200 ml/¾ cup full-fat/ whole milk

300 ml/1¼ cups condensed milk

a pinch of saffron strands

¼ teaspoon ground cardamom

1 tablespoon caster/ granulated sugar

4 tablespoons (dark) raisins

5 tablespoons chopped pistachio nuts

100 g/¾ cup plain/ all-purpose flour

1 pack of filo/phyllo pastry (250 g/9 oz.)

ice cream, to serve

baking sheet, lined with baking parchment

SERVES 10
(MAKES 30 SAMOSAS)

Heat the ghee in a pan over low heat and sauté the grated carrot for 20 minutes or until well softened.

Add the milk and reduce by half over low heat. This will take about 30 minutes, so be patient and keep stirring occasionally.

Add the condensed milk and saffron and simmer for a further 15 minutes. Add the ground cardamom, sugar, (dark) raisins and pistachio nuts and mix well.

Transfer to a shallow, chilling container and place in the refrigerator to cool and chill.

While it is chilling, prepare the flour glue by whisking the flour and 200 ml/ ¾ cup of water together.

Preheat the oven to 170°C (325°F) Gas 3.

Cut the filo/phyllo sheets into 30 rectangles measuring 25 x 8 cm/ 10 x 3¼ inches. Keep the pastry covered until required.

When the filling has chilled, place roughly 30 g/1 oz. of filling at one end of a pastry rectangle. Take the right corner and fold diagonally to the left, enclosing the filling and forming a triangle. Fold again along the upper crease of the triangle. Keep folding this way until you are left with a little strip of pastry at the end. Brush a little of the flour glue on the exposed bit of pastry, then fold over and enclose the samosa completely. Repeat to make 30 samosas.

Place all of the samosas on the prepared baking sheet and bake in the preheated oven for 15 minutes, turning them over after 5 minutes or so.

Serve the samosas warm with ice cream.

DARJEELING CHAI PANNA COTTA

My chai panna cotta makes the perfect end to a meal when you want to really impress your guests. Panna cotta is a traditional Italian dessert consisting of set sweetened cream – I love it and I wanted to apply my modern Indian twist to the Italian classic. As a huge tea fan, I have a large collection of regional teas, and one variety, which always sticks out for me, is Darjeeling tea. Darjeeling is a town in west Bengal and is famous for its tea industry. Darjeeling tea, also referred to as the 'Champagne of tea', has a floral aroma with a musky taste, which goes well with the richness of the set cream.

3 gelatine leaves
250 ml/1 cup double/
   heavy cream
250 ml/1 cup semi-
   skimmed milk
50 g/¼ cup caster/
   granulated sugar
4 Darjeeling masala
   chai teabags
2–3 cardamom pods
2–3 cloves
a 5-cm/2-inch
   cinnamon stick

SERVES 6

Put the gelatine leaves in cold water and allow to soften.

Place the cream, milk, sugar, teabags and all of the whole spices in a pan. Gently bring to the boil, then reduce the heat and simmer for 10 minutes. Strain the mixture and discard the teabags and whole spices. Return the infused cream mixture back to the heat.

Gently squeeze the soaked gelatine leaves to remove any excess water, add them to the pan and whisk in the gelatine leaves until they have melted into the cream mixture.

Gently transfer the panna cotta mixture into a pouring jug/pitcher and then pour the mixture into the desired serving dishes. I like to use coffee cups or glasses.

Chill in the refrigerator until set. This will depend on the serving dish you choose, but should take no longer than 5 hours. For best results, set overnight.

I like to serve them in the cups, but if you want to serve your panna cottas on a plate, you will have to remove them from the moulds or cups. To do this, briefly dip the base of the moulds in hot water (careful not to get any water on the actual panna cotta) and use a blunt knife to gently loosen the edges.

AN INDIAN SUMMER NIGHT'S DREAM

When I was a child, I was fascinated with the Shakespeare play, 'A Midsummer Night's Dream'. I loved the magical, fairyland setting and that is a concept that I wanted to pay tribute to, and so here is My Indian Summer Night's Dream. The dessert is almost like the British Eton Mess but with the addition of black pepper in the meringue and using mango rather than fresh summer berries. It's not meant to be a 'prim and proper' plated dessert but more of a rustic one-bowl delight. Enjoy!

1 mango, peeled, stoned/pitted and roughly diced

BLACK PEPPER MERINGUE
3 egg whites
120 g/scant ⅔ cup caster/granulated sugar
a pinch of salt
a pinch of crushed black pepper

MINTED CREAM
500 ml/2 cups double/heavy cream
100 ml/⅓ cup mango purée
5–6 mint leaves, finely chopped

baking sheet, lined with baking parchment

SERVES 5

Preheat the oven to 150°C (300°F) Gas 2.

Make the meringue. In a clean bowl, whisk the egg whites to stiff peaks using an electric handheld whisk.

Gradually (this can take a while) add the sugar and salt and whisk for 6 minutes on a medium setting until smooth and glossy. Add the pinch of black pepper and gently fold through.

Spread the meringue mix flat across the lined baking sheet using a palette knife or metal spatula so that the meringue is evenly spread.

Bake the meringue in the preheated oven for 5 minutes and then switch off the oven. Leave the meringue in the oven to finish cooking for 55 minutes. Transfer to a wire rack to cool.

Make the minted cream by whisking the double/heavy cream in a bowl until it forms soft peaks and holds its shape when the whisk is removed. Gently fold in the mango purée and chopped mint, then put in the refrigerator until required.

Break the meringue apart into small bite-sized chunks. Assemble the dessert by mixing the cooled black pepper meringue, the minted cream and chopped mango together. Serve immediately.

CHILLI/CHILE AND PINEAPPLE TARTS

I took inspiration for this recipe from my time spent in the pastry section of a hotel I once to worked in. It has more of a European influence with the use of the puff pastry, but the combination of pineapple and chilli/chile adds a tropical appeal to the dessert. The heat of the fresh chilli/chile pairs well with the sweetness of the pineapple and caramel sauce. I serve it with whipped cream and chopped mint leaves if I want it to look pretty.

1 pineapple, peeled and eyes and central core removed
2 large sheets of ready-rolled puff pastry (320 g/ 11 oz. each)
1 red chilli/chile, finely diced (seeds removed)
whipped cream or ice cream, to serve

CARAMEL SAUCE
200 g/1 cup caster/ granulated sugar
2 star anise
120 g/1 stick unsalted butter

10 mini tart pans, about 12 cm/4½ inch diameter

SERVES 10

Preheat the oven to 190°C (375°F) Gas 5.

Cut the peeled pineapple into 10 equal slices and set aside until required.

Using the mini tart pans (making sure they are big enough to fit a slice of pineapple in the bottom), cut out 10 pastry lids by using the top of a tart pan as a template. The pastry lids should be around 5 mm/¼ inch thick. Place the pastry lids on a sheet of baking parchment with another sheet on top to stop them from drying out.

Sprinkle a little bit of the chilli/chile in the bottom of each individual tart pan and set aside until required.

For the caramel sauce, heat a large frying pan/skillet over medium heat, add the sugar and star anise and heat gently until you have a light caramel. Stir gently using a wooden spoon and be careful not to touch the caramel.

Add the slices of pineapple and cook on each side for no longer than 1 minute. The pineapple slices should release some natural juices into the sugar syrup creating a lovely base for the caramel sauce.

Remove the frying pan/skillet from the heat and place a sealed slice of pineapple in each individual tart pan, retaining as much of the sauce in the frying pan/skillet as possible.

Return the frying pan/skillet to the heat and add the butter. Mix well to create a lovely rich and sweet caramel sauce. Divide the sauce equally between the tart pans and shake them a little to distribute the sauce.

Cover each slice of caramelized pineapple with a pastry lid and tuck in the edges around the pineapple slice. Place all of the tarts onto a baking sheet and bake in the preheated oven for 20–25 minutes until the pastry is golden-brown.

Serve the tarts while still warm with a dollop of whipped cream on top.

CHOCOLATE AND MADRAS COFFEE CAKE

What would a dessert selection be without a chocolate cake? And what goes well with chocolate cake – coffee! I am a fan of both coffee and chocolate and wanted a dessert that celebrates both, but with a modern Indian twist. A few years ago, I came across a lovely subtle south Indian coffee from Madras that delivered a great flavour but didn't have the effects of caffeine. Finished with a cardamom frosting, this cake not only makes a great after-dinner treat but also a lovely little delicacy to be enjoyed with afternoon tea.

COFFEE MIX
½ teaspoon south Indian filter coffee (or other good-quality coffee)
¼ teaspoon ground cardamom
200 ml/¾ cup boiling water

CAKE MIXTURE
125 g/4 oz. dark/bittersweet chocolate
125 g/1 stick plus 1 tablespoon unsalted butter
75 g/scant ⅔ cup self-raising/self-rising flour, sifted
75 g/scant ⅔ cup plain/all-purpose flour, sifted
¼ teaspoon bicarbonate of soda/baking soda
40 g/generous ⅓ cup unsweetened cocoa powder

250 g/1¼ cups caster/granulated sugar
2 eggs
1 tablespoon sunflower oil
50 ml/3½ tablespoons full-fat/whole milk

FROSTING
200 g/1¾ sticks unsalted butter
200 g/1½ cups icing/confectioners' sugar
10 g/1½ tablespoons cocoa powder
a pinch of ground cardamom

TO DECORATE
chocolate shavings

2 x 23-cm/9-inch cake pans, greased and lined with baking parchment

SERVES 10

For the coffee mix, place the filter coffee and cardamom powder in a measuring jug/cup and pour over the boiling water. Allow to brew for 5–6 minutes, then strain. Set aside to cool.

Preheat the oven to 170°C (325°F) Gas 3.

For the cake, melt the chocolate and butter in a heatproof bowl set over a pan of barely simmering water. Make sure the bottom of the bowl does not touch the water. Stir until the mixture is completely melted, then remove the bowl and mix in 2 tablespoons of the coffee mixture. Set aside.

In another large mixing bowl, mix together the two flours, the bicarbonate of soda/baking soda, cocoa powder and sugar. Make a well in the middle.

Beat the eggs, oil and milk together and whisk into the well of the dry ingredients. Mix well to bring all of the ingredients together. Pour in the melted chocolate, butter and coffee mixture and mix to combine.

Divide the mixture between the cake pans and bake in the preheated oven for 30 minutes or until a skewer inserted into the cakes comes out clean. Cool completely before removing from the pans.

To make the frosting, mix together the butter, icing/confectioners' sugar, cocoa powder and cardamom powder with 2 tablespoons of the strained coffee mix. When the cakes have cooled, coat them in the frosting using a palette knife. Decorate with a sprinkle of chocolate shavings.

INDEX

ACKNOWLEDGMENTS

A special thank you to my family and friends, for their constant love and support over the years. They have always pushed me to achieve my dreams and ambitions.

Most importantly, my mother, who was by my side every day of writing this book. Whether it was preparing ingredients, washing up dishes or giving her advice on recipes, I could not have done this without her.

Thank you to all the team at Ryland, Peters & Small: Stephanie Milner, Megan Smith, Leslie Harrington, Julia Charles, Abi Waters, Cindy Richards and David Hearn; it's strange to believe how the book has been brought to life so beautifully in just a matter of months! To the photography team, Emily Kydd, Jennifer Kay and Clare Winfield – you really all have done such a great job and I'm so happy with every single aspect of it.